Praise for **All Fired Up**

"Reading this book makes me want to get a copy for everyone at my company."
DON WILLIAMSON, president, Oak House Benefits

"*All Fired Up* is a master class in optimizing mental health to unlock joy. Anthony is a gifted and down-to-earth storyteller who empowers readers, from boardrooms to personal lives, to discover our unique rhythm where we can excel at work and still make time to reenergize. A must-read for those striving to maximize peak performance."
CURTIS CARMICHAEL, award-winning STEAM teacher and author

"Instantly applicable and endlessly empowering, *All Fired Up* is a game-changer for those aiming to optimize their productivity and overall well-being."
HAILEY HECHTMAN, executive director, Unsinkable

"Anthony wrote a validating and energizing book to lift us up in this busy time. A wonderful reassurance that we're stronger than we think, and that we can still be OK when life gets turbulent."
JESSICA HOLMES, comedian and mental health advocate

"In this uplifting book, Anthony teaches a self-care-centered approach to building your own unique set of mental wellness tools that will improve your day-to-day productivity, creativity, and energy levels."
EMILY SORLIE, executive producer, Stature Films

"In *All Fired Up*, Anthony McLean has laid out the path to sustainable personal and professional thriving. Synthesizing the compassion of holistic wellness practices with the focus and drive of an entrepreneur, Anthony has given us a toolkit that is practical, equitable, hopeful, and results-driven. Frankly, it's a breath of fresh air in the self-help genre!"
JONATHAN PUDDLE, spirituality coach and author

Optimize Mental Wellness to Ignite Joy and Fuel Peak Performance

ALL FIRED UP

ANTHONY MCLEAN

Copyright © 2024 by Anthony McLean

All rights reserved. No part of this book may be reproduced, stored in a retrieval system or transmitted, in any form or by any means, without the prior written consent of the publisher, except in the case of brief quotations, embodied in reviews and articles.

This book is not intended as a substitute for the medical advice of physicians. The reader should regularly consult a physician in matters relating to his/her/their health and particularly with respect to any symptoms that may require diagnosis or medical attention.

Cataloguing in publication information is available from Library and Archives Canada.
ISBN 978-1-77458-397-5 (paperback)
ISBN 978-1-77458-398-2 (ebook)

Page Two
pagetwo.com

Edited by Emily Schultz and Kendra Ward
Copyedited by Rachel Taylor
Proofread by Rachel Ironstone
Cover and interior design by Fiona Lee

anthonymclean.org/book

*For Susie, Josh, and Ariella.
You're the reason I'm so fired up!*

THE FUEL TO FIRE UP

Looking for the contents? Flip a few pages ahead. Otherwise, start your journey here:

As soon as you start exploring self-improvement, you're pulled in two directions by two well-meaning groups. One group tells you hustle harder. Wake up at four in the morning and grind until midnight. They want you to make productivity the priority. We'll call this group the "motivation squad." The other group will tell you to put on an eye mask, run a hot bath, and enjoy some scented candles. This crowd wants you to make self-care a priority. We'll call these folks the "wellness circle." These two groups seem to be at odds with each other. And that's a shame, because they don't need to be. In fact, I've adapted tools from both groups that resulted in the book you're holding.

When I set out to write this book, I just wanted a clear answer to these simple questions: How can I spend more time in peak performance? How can I have more energy to do what I love and to be present with the people that I love?

Like you, I have ambitious goals for my career, and I wanted to figure out how to make the most of my workday.

You know those days when you are alert, focused, and productive?

- You have the energy to get your work done.
- You're clear about your goals and stay on task.
- You're motivated to tackle your to-do list.

That's what I call the peak performance zone. I love being in the zone. I wish I felt like that every day. But...

You know those days when you are sluggish, lethargic, and unmotivated?

- You don't want to look at your to-do list.
- You've lost all enthusiasm for work.
- You can't seem to stay on task.

I call that "the blahs." And I wanted to bust the blahs and sharpen my focus, boost my energy, and spend more time in peak performance. So I set out to find the tools that would work for me. But a funny thing happened.

I discovered that operating at your full potential is a by-product of tried-and-true mental health habits. Getting eight hours of sleep improves cognitive function. Staying hydrated keeps you energized. Practicing meditation increases attention span, creative thinking, and problem-solving skills.

If you want to white-knuckle your way through your career, you can ignore your mental health and grind yourself down. But if you want a well-rounded life, with vibrant, energizing relationships, rich personal time, and a sustainable pace at work, then being intentional about your mental health is nonnegotiable. Many of the high performers we admire are in the fast lane to burnout. They're working at an unhealthy, unsustainable, unrealistic pace. I don't want that for myself. And I don't want that for you!

What Does It Mean to Be All Fired Up?

Being All Fired Up means discovering your own personal rhythm where you crush it at work and you make time to refuel and rejuvenate. It means being as motivated to achieve career success as you are committed to self-care. To be All Fired Up, you must be all fueled up. And good mental health habits are the fuel that will take you to your goals.

I've seen too many people sacrifice their health and their closest relationships in pursuit of a better title, a bigger office, or some shiny award. I'm not willing to do that. Yes, I want professional success, but I also want to live a good life! Let me explain why this is important to me.

My career is a bit unconventional in that I've got my feet in two worlds. In the corporate world, I'm a keynote speaker for Fortune 500 companies. I speak at between fifty and a hundred events each year and go through layers of preparation for each event: meetings, emails, working out logistics with event planners, research, travel... It's a lot. But it's all worth it. Every time I step on stage, I feel a rush of adrenaline. I'm grateful for the opportunity to share life-changing ideas with people all over the world. I love this work!

The other part of my career is in the entertainment industry. I moved to Los Angeles to pursue my goals as a screenwriter. It's going well, but it's not without its challenges. I'm in development on two feature films right now and I'm writing a third. I do pitch meetings with Hollywood executives, work with producers and investors to secure funding, and write alongside a robust writers' group that meets five hours each week. I love being a screenwriter! And although my career may seem unconventional, it happened pretty naturally.

As a kid, I was always performing. In elementary school, I got a reputation for being the class clown. Most teachers found me

Good mental health habits benefit everyone with a brain. (And everyone in their immediate sphere!)

disruptive, but one teacher saw me differently: my sixth-grade English teacher, Ms. Hepburn. She told me I needed a stage. She encouraged my mom to enroll me in a speech and drama class with a brilliant acting coach named Tessa. Every Tuesday night, my mom drove me down to Tessa's studio where I performed monologues, recited poems, and improvised hilarious sketches, all without derailing a math lesson. I loved every minute of it.

Soon, I was booking commercials and small TV shows. After high school, I was offered the opportunity to perform Shakespeare at the renowned Stratford Festival in Ontario, Canada. Later, I was cast as the host of an after-school program on CBC Television (Canada's national broadcaster). I got to work with incredible people like Ryan Reynolds, Drake, Tina Fey, and more. To promote the show, we traveled to schools across the country. A school would bring the entire student population down to the gymnasium, hand me the microphone, and I'd perform for half an hour. I told stories, cracked jokes, and even freestyle rapped at these performances. It was a blast!

After one of these shows, a guidance counselor approached me and said, "The kids love you! Our biggest problem right now is bullying. Could you come back and do a session about that?"

That request changed the direction of my life. I started reading all the material I could find. I got really stirred up when I realized that bullying is oppression on a small scale—it's one kid using a power advantage to hurt another. I became a bullying prevention advocate and spoke in schools across the country. My calendar was so full that I put acting aside to become a full-time speaker. Looking back, it's hard to believe that I've connected with students in over two thousand schools in Canada, the United States, and Australia.

In addition to speaking about bullying, I began talks on diversity, inclusion, and mental health. These topics are close to my heart, and the work felt effective, timely, and rewarding. I wrote screenplays to satisfy my creative appetite and I delivered presentations about important issues to make an impact in the world. From that time until now, speaking and screenwriting have been my two passions.

But there was a problem. Some days when I showed up for a talk, I was in the peak performance zone—energized, focused, and ready to take the stage. But other days, I had the blahs—I felt sluggish, lethargic, and unmotivated. Instead of being an inspirational speaker, I was the one who needed inspiration! And the frustrating part was, I didn't know why I was in peak performance on one day and in the blahs on another.

I had the same problem in my creative life. I'd block out several hours to work on a screenplay, and some days I'd be at peak performance—alert, creative, and energized. Other days, the blahs descended, and I couldn't write a single page! Why was I focused on Monday and floundering on Tuesday?

To make matters worse, when I gave 100 percent at work, I'd return home to my family with an empty tank. This put me in a tight spot. I wasn't willing to sacrifice my career, and I wasn't willing to be half-hearted with my family. I needed to find a way to operate at peak performance without burning out. I needed to learn how to be All Fired Up! The good news is that the tools that worked for me are in the chapters ahead. And because I work in different worlds, I can promise you: these tools translate to all industries, at all levels.

This Book Is about You

I want to give you permission to read this book in any order you'd like. That's the reason why you haven't seen the contents page yet. It's coming up in a few pages. Give it a look and see where you'd like to begin. Maybe you need some insight on dealing with failure, developing confidence, or handling hard days. Ultimately, this book is about you. If a subject feels too heavy, don't explore it today. If another feels especially relevant, perhaps that's where you begin. Choose your own adventure! This is all about building up your mental health. Speaking of which, let's unpack the term "mental health."

Mental health includes your mood, your emotions, and your ability to think clearly. It directly affects your energy levels, your drive, and your passion for life. Your sense of well-being, your ability to pursue goals, and your coping skills for tough times are all related to your mental health. Everyone has mental health, but not everyone is intentional about taking care of their mental health.

Often, we confuse "mental health" with "mental illness." Some people think that being mindful of mental health is only relevant for people with a diagnosed mental illness. That's like saying exercise only benefits people with an injury. The truth is that exercise benefits everyone with a body. And good mental health habits benefit everyone with a brain. (And everyone in their immediate sphere!)

In 2021, an estimated one in five adults in the United States were living with mental illness. We need to normalize the conversation surrounding mental illness. It's not a weakness, a lack of discipline, or something that goes away after a bath or a nap—it's an illness.

Let me take this one step further. Have you ever gone for a run and felt your muscles burning? You know that you're not injured—you want to push through the discomfort to make it to your finish line.

Now imagine that you and a friend go on a run. Halfway to your goal, your friend says her leg hurts. You tell her to ignore it, to push through the pain. You assume you know her pain—her muscles are burning. But what if she's sprained an ankle? If she's injured, your advice to push through the pain isn't helpful, it's hurtful. And it will make her injury even worse.

It's the same with a person with a mental illness. They have an injury that needs proper treatment, and the world keeps telling them to "walk it off." I don't want to be part of that. We will explore some truly helpful tools in this book. But please don't offer these as a cure for a mental illness.

One more caveat before we dive in. I'm an advocate for mental health. I'm not a doctor, practitioner, or a clinician. I'm passionate about mental health because I've experienced a massive improvement in both my performance at work and my well-being at home when I'm intentional about my wellness routines. For me, mental health has been a game-changer. I believe it will be for you too! The material in this book is backed by science and research, but it is not medical advice. As always, talk to a doctor before you implement any health plan.

OK, now that we've got that out of the way, let's get you All Fired Up! Check out the contents on the next page and let's begin the journey to a happier, healthier, more resilient you!

CONTENTS

The Fuel to Fire Up ix

1. **Hustle Culture, Meet Self-Care** 1
2. **Finding the Balance** 17
3. **Making Time for Joy** 33
4. **How to Handle Hard Days** 47
5. **The Power of Self-Awareness** 61
6. **Dealing with Anxiety** 73
7. **The Body-Brain Connection** 87
8. **The Confidence Factor** 103
9. **Relationships** 115
10. **Facing Failure** 131
11. **Excuseless** 147

Conclusion 159
Acknowledgments 161
Notes 165

1

HUSTLE CULTURE, MEET SELF-CARE

It is not enough to be busy.
So are the ants. The question is:
What are we busy about?

HENRY DAVID THOREAU

MY SOCIAL media feed is populated by the "motivation squad" and the "wellness circle." Both focus on self-improvement, but they take very different approaches. The core message from the motivation squad (or as some might call it, "hustle culture") is about maximizing your time, your money, and your productivity so you can see exponential results. These folks will have you excited about waking up before dawn, jumping into a cold shower, and running a marathon all before the workday begins. They motivate you to go out and crush your goals. As much as I love the motivation squad, there's definitely a dark side. Left unchecked, this kind of hustle can lead to burnout. A race car that doesn't get enough pit stops will run out of gas.

The wellness circle are a much gentler bunch. They primarily focus on self-care, well-being, and personal reflection. I love the wellness circle. They remind me to tune into my feelings, resist the urge to rush, and eliminate all sources of stress to cultivate a perfectly peaceful mindset. But taken to the extreme, their advice leads to a lot of self-absorption without any tangible progress. A race car that spends too much time in the pit stop will never win the race.

What we all need is a bridge between these two communities. We need to nurture ourselves so that we have the energy to do great work.

The approach of *All Fired Up!* is about taking the best of both these worlds to fuel your peak performance. It's about practicing self-care so that you can pursue your big, hairy, audacious goals—but not at the expense of your well-being. It's about practicing meditation at lunch so you can crush it in the afternoon. It's about striking a healthy work-life balance for a holistic, sustainable lifestyle. It's about how to consistently give your best, year after year, without burning out.

When I first set out to write this book, I was only interested in improving my workday performance. I knew who I was in my peak performance zone: a focused, alert, clear-thinking, creative problem-solver with the energy and motivation to stay on task. But I also found those moments to be fleeting and unpredictable. I wanted a reliable on-ramp to peak performance. The good news is that I discovered many on-ramps. What surprised me was that every on-ramp required me to step up my mental health skills.

This dynamic reminds me of Aesop's fable about the golden goose. You remember that one, right? A farmer stumbles upon a goose that lays one solid gold egg every single day. Amazing! But there's a problem: this farmer is a member of the motivation squad! He's keen to "10X" his profit margins. So instead of waiting patiently, he guts the goose, expecting a gold mine inside. Instead, all he's left with is a bloody mess. It's awful. The poor goose dies, and the farmer never sees another golden egg. The moral of the story: if you want golden eggs, you've got to take care of the goose! And if you want peak performance, you've got to take care of your mental health habits. (And leave those geese alone!)

I delved into a mountain of research that reaffirmed my lived experience—daily habits will enable you to spend more time in your peak performance zone. And if you take time to recharge and replenish throughout the day, you'll return home with energy for friends, family, and personal time. In the chapters ahead, you'll find habits and tools, rhythms and routines that will help you to be at your best, for the longest amount of time, with the least amount of wear and tear. Some of these tools may seem silly, but if they help you thrive, who cares?! When you discover what you personally need to be at your best, your productivity will skyrocket, your creative juices will flow, and you'll be happier at work and at home.

The Gift of Self-Acceptance

Some of us have been conditioned to be attuned to the needs of others while ignoring our own needs. If that feels familiar, you're not alone. At first, it was strange for me to focus on myself. It was like brushing my teeth with my nondominant hand. But, over time, I improved my productivity and boosted my sense of wellness. So, I encourage you not to shrink back from exploring these tools. The more honest you are in examining what is and isn't working for you, the more effective these on-ramps will be.

Before I share some of the tools that have worked for me, let me be clear: being All Fired Up is not a one-size-fits-all approach. Not all these tools will fit your lifestyle without some modifications. We all have unique roles, responsibilities, health considerations, energy levels, and home and work environments that change over time. Be kind to yourself as you explore a new habit or routine. You might find journaling helpful to record how you feel as you implement different tools.

All right, here we go! I'm going to share some of the habits that have helped me unlock my full potential. I hope it sparks some curiosity about what may get you All Fired Up! The first is about peak performance times.

When Are You at Your Best?

Your energy levels fluctuate throughout the day. Some people feel a surge of creativity at night. Others feel most productive in the morning. How about you? When in the day are you at your best in terms of energy? When do you do your best thinking? Can you plan your day so that you are doing your most important work when your energy is at its highest?

One task you probably don't want to do during your peak performance time is read emails.

For many, emails are an energy drain. They feel important, but the truth is, they can usually wait until after lunch. If your job depends entirely on responding to emails promptly, please ignore this. But for the rest of us, take this good advice from a friend of mine who is a prolific artist: ignore your emails as much as you can without getting yourself in trouble. What would happen if you only responded to emails twice a day? Once at noon and again at four in the afternoon? Why not give it a try? And if possible, don't schedule emails during your peak performance time.

I do my best work in the morning before I check email or social media. Ideally, I'd love to wake up early and write, but my kids get up at six for school so the mornings are busy. I drop them off at the bus stop at 7:30 and I'm at my work-from-home desk at eight. From eight until ten I try not to even peek at emails. I don't check the news or open any social media. Those two hours, when my mind is clear and I'm blissfully unaware of the demands of the outside world, are when I do my best work. At the end of each workday I answer the question: What is important right now? And the next day, those two hours are dedicated to that important stuff. Some days I'm traveling and I don't get that two-hour window. Some days I'm speaking at an event at eight in the morning and I don't get that window. But whenever possible, I keep those two hours clear on my calendar.

What about you? When do you do your best work? When do you come up with your best ideas? When do you feel most decisive? Is it first thing in the morning? Is it after lunch? Is it late at night? You need to guard that window of time as best you can and schedule your most important work during that time.

A little movement: Here's what works for me. I share it with you to spark curiosity about what you might need to be in your peak performance zone.

When I'm writing, I need to move around. Every hour, I like to stand up and stretch. I will do some arm circles or jumping jacks. I might bounce around on a rebounder (a small trampoline). I also alternate between sitting at my desk and standing at my desk. I've worked at a beautiful motorized electric desk that raises up at the push of a button. (Shout-out to my friends Andrew and Emily Sorlie who play the song "You Raise Me Up" by Josh Groban every time they raise their desk!) I've also used a less elegant version of the stand-up desk consisting of a stack of cardboard boxes on top of a regular desk. Either way, I don't like to sit for too long. So, alternating between sitting and standing is important for me.

A creative walk: The other secret for me to be in my peak performance zone is the creative walk. Two or three times a day, I'll walk around the block and take in the sky, the trees, the fresh air to inspire me. Something about the rhythm of walking enhances my creative thinking. If I'm stuck on an idea, if I'm fired up about an idea, or if I'm just tired of looking at my computer screen, I'll put on my running shoes and go for a fifteen-minute walk.

A little caffeine: If I don't have caffeine in the morning, I'm not in my peak performance zone. I used to feel guilty about that. I really wanted to be one of those people (like my wife, Susie!)

who don't need caffeine to function. I felt weak for needing an outside substance to make me feel at my best. But now, I've made peace with it. I try not to overdo my caffeine intake, and I'll even try to go a few days without caffeine every now and then, but I also don't beat myself up for loving coffee!

Pavlovian bells: Remember Pavlov's dogs? Pavlov rang a bell every time he fed his dogs. Soon enough, the sound of a bell ringing got the dogs salivating and looking for food. By establishing associations, your brain becomes primed for productive tasks. If there's a specific drink that you only have when it's time to work, your brain will associate that drink with work! Maybe there's a certain sound, like 30 Hz binaural beats, that you exclusively listen to when you're diving into work mode. Whether it's a scented candle, a particular spot in your living or working space, or even a distinct flavor of gum that you only chew when you work, your brain will pick up on these cues for when it's time to shift into work mode.

One Tool, Dozens of Benefits

We all have different tools to be at our best. But I'd like to suggest one tool that helps improve focus, mood, and cognitive function. This tool is backed by thousands of years of practice in cultures throughout the world. And this tool is backed by thousands of brain studies that have scientifically proven its effectiveness.

This tool is meditation.

If you want to spend more time in your peak performance zone, a daily meditation practice is a great place to start.

One study placed people into two groups, one which listened to an uplifting podcast for thirteen minutes a day, the

The more honest you are in examining what works for you, the more effective these on-ramps to mental health and peak performance will be.

other which practiced meditation for thirteen minutes a day. For eight weeks, the researchers examined the effects on the participants' mood, memory, cognitive function, cortisol levels, and emotional regulation. The group that practiced meditation outperformed the podcast listeners in attention, memory, mood, and cognitive function, and had decreased anxiety.

We often think we need to hustle more to achieve more. This study suggests that sometimes you get further by slowing down.

Maybe you've already read the research on the benefits of meditation and you're meditating daily. Or maybe you've been hesitant because you think meditation is a little too spiritual for you. The meditation I'm talking about is not spiritual. It's brain science. Meditation is slowing down, setting an intentional focus, and trying not to think about anything else.

Full disclosure: if you are like me, as soon as you try not to think about anything else, you will find yourself thinking about everything else! You'll try to focus on your breath but find yourself thinking about your grocery list or your knee pain or your sudden desire to tidy up your desk. When that happens, it's no big deal, you simply observe the thought, let it go, and reset your intention.

Don't give yourself a hard time if your focus constantly drifts. The act of noticing your focus drifting and then refocusing on your intention strengthens your cognitive functions.

Don't be a critic when you meditate. Be an observer.

There are a many different types of meditation, but I'll focus on four: box breathing, listening for silence, observing nature, and practicing a simple mantra.

Box Breathing

Sit or lie down comfortably. With your eyes closed:

- Breathe in for four seconds.
- Hold your breath for four seconds.
- Breathe out for four seconds.
- Hold your breath for four seconds.

Some people visualize an imaginary box and trace its lines with their fingers while they breathe—hence the term "box breathing." Try box breathing for three to five minutes. Box breathing is a great way to reset your mind as you switch tasks. When I'm moving from emails to creative work, three minutes of box breathing helps me get a fresh new focus.

Listening for Silence

Sit or lie comfortably with your eyes closed. Focus your attention on all the sounds around you:

- Notice the hum of the refrigerator.
- Hear an airplane in the distance.
- Listen to the sound of your own breathing.
- Observe the ticking of a clock.
- Note the sound of cars in the street.

Now listen for another sound in the midst of it all: the sound of silence. (No, not the Simon & Garfunkel song!) I want you to listen for the silence amid all the noise. Let me explain...

In film editing software, there are several layers of audio. One layer of audio has an actor's dialogue, another layer has music, and another layer has sound effects. Since each layer of audio is recorded separately, the sound mixer can mute individual layers and just listen to the actor's dialogue. Or they can mute the actor's dialogue and just listen to the sound effects. It's pretty cool.

There is a layer of audio in every sound mix called "room tone." It's basically the sound of silence within the scene. Every room has its own sound of silence. The silence in a large concert hall is very different from the silence in your bathroom. And even in a noisy room, a layer of audio is simply silence. I want you to start listening for that silence.

Let's try this one right now. Close your eyes for thirty seconds and listen to all the sounds around you. Try to detect the "room tone" behind all the other sounds. Can you find the silence?

I love listening for silence because it teaches me that when my thoughts are swirling and I feel overwhelmed, if I slow down and listen, a stillness and silence in my own mind is always accessible.

Observing Nature

Whenever I spend time in nature, I always feel revitalized in my soul. I love going for a walk through the woods or gazing at the stars at night or sitting on the beach watching the waves crash.

I love a good sunset.

I love watching bees burrowing into flowers.

I love watching hawks soaring peacefully through the skies, and I love watching squirrels bickering with each other over acorns. Nature is a constant performance... if we are paying attention. And to be fully immersed in observing nature is a form of meditation that is super rejuvenating.

So, get outside. Study a snowflake. Go bird-watching! Look at a spider spinning a web. Watch a snail moving through the grass. Lie in the grass and stare at the clouds. Turn off your phone, ignore your to-do list, and be fully absorbed in the majesty of Mother Nature.

Not only is time in nature a delight to your senses, but it's good for your mental health. Numerous studies have proven that time in nature can boost your mood, improve your ability to focus, and reduce risk of depression and other mood disorders. So, get outside and take it in. You'll be glad you did!

Practicing a Mantra

In Hinduism and Buddhism, mantras are an important spiritual practice. And medical researchers have proven that repeating a soothing phrase while meditating can reduce symptoms of depression.

Personally, I have had amazing results from meditating with a single encouraging phrase, or a promise from the bible, or a lesson I learned from therapy. When my focus drifts, I observe it without judgment and bring my focus back to the mantra. It is powerful!

What "aha" moment have you had recently that you need to remember? What emotional breakthrough do you want to hold close to your heart? In an age when we consume information in mass amounts, slowing down and meditating on one solid piece of wisdom is helpful.

Sometimes, I'll use a mantra for a day or two. Other times, I might need the same mantra for a week or more. Give it a try. Set a five-minute timer, close your eyes, and repeat one phrase over and over again. Here are a few examples.

Mantras for confidence:
- I feel the fear and persist.
- I don't need to impress anyone.
- What others think of me is none of my business.
- My future is amazing.

(Shout-out to Gabi Garcia and Glennon Doyle!)

Mantras for anxiety:
- I am safe; I am secure.
- Fear does not control me.
- Calm washes over me.
- This too shall pass.
- I release my grip on what I cannot control.

Mantras for depression:
- Feelings are temporary.
- Even now, there is joy to be found.
- This too shall pass.
- Good things await me.
- I am worthy of a good life.

I have found meditation to be one of the most beneficial mental health practices of all. It's a game-changer! And you don't need a robust meditation practice to reap the results. Studies have shown benefits from as little as three minutes of daily meditation. And that can be one tool to help with work-life balance.

No One-Size-Fits-All Approach

Let me gently emphasize that when it comes to managing mental well-being, there's no universal, one-size-fits-all solution. If you've experienced severe trauma in the past, certain mindfulness practices like meditation or breathwork might feel more daunting than soothing—and that's perfectly OK. It's crucial to remember that you should move at your own pace and find strategies that resonate with you personally.

In some cases, the most effective step might be seeking help from a professional therapist or counselor, who can provide personalized guidance suited to your unique situation. Some people may find a therapist with expertise in somatic or embodiment therapies especially helpful. What's most important is understanding that you're worth it—you truly deserve the right care and treatment for your well-being.

GET ALL FIRED UP!

Optimize mental wellness: Give yourself the gift of self-acceptance. Get curious about what life or work habits and simple activities improve your energy levels.

Ignite joy: Choose an activity that makes you feel alive (I suggested a little movement, a little caffeine, and other possibilities, but do what works for you). Incorporate it into one day this week and see how you feel. In what ways does it give you a boost?

Fuel peak performance: Slow down and refuel. Try one of the four meditations I describe in this chapter. Or just breathe. Just breathe.

2

FINDING THE BALANCE

A perfect work-life balance is like a perfect haircut. As soon as you think you have it, it starts growing out of control again.

ANONYMOUS

DON'T KNOW anyone who has a perfect balance between work life and home life on any given day. And I think that's OK.

Nature has seasons, and so do we. If you are an accountant, tax time is a busy season for work. That's not when you'll be going on a family vacation or taking up a new hobby. But that doesn't mean you are unbalanced—you're just in a busy work season.

On the other hand, if you go on a two-week camping trip with your family, you won't be keeping up with emails. And that's to be expected! Remember—there is a season for everything. Look for balance in the year, not in the days.

The Balance of Stress and Rest

Think about the way your body becomes stronger. During exercise, your muscles are under stress. This stress puts rips and tears in the muscle fiber. Then, when you rest and get some protein, the tears in your muscle fibers are repaired, which ends up making you stronger.

If you put too much stress on your body, you'll get injured. If you rest your body for too long, you'll lose your strength.

It's all about balance. And it's the same for your mental wellness. You don't need to avoid stress. You need an appropriate amount of rest for your level of stress. Stress + Rest = Blessed.

STRESS + **REST** = **BLESSED**

You can handle stress, as long as you get enough rest. You can handle challenges, as long as you get enough rest. You can do hard things, as long as you get enough rest. As singer, actress, and activist Lena Horne said, "It's not the load that breaks you down, it's the way you carry it." And that means embracing rest as an essential part of your work-life balance.

The same way a race car driver will pull over for a pit stop to refuel, I want you to develop a pattern of going hard, pulling over to recover, and then going hard again.

The Turtle and the Rabbit

I love Aesop's fable about the tortoise and the hare. But I'd like to revisit this story for two reasons:

1 I think we need to rename it "The Turtle and the Rabbit," for simplicity's sake.

2 We need to take another look at the moral of the story.

You remember the story, right? A rabbit and a turtle decide to race. The rabbit takes off in a hurry! She is one hundred yards ahead of the turtle, who is moving slow and steady. The rabbit finally looks back, sees the lead she has on the turtle, and says to herself, "I'm way in front. I'm going to have a nap." And she falls asleep right there on the track. While she sleeps, the turtle just keeps moving, slow and steady, and eventually wins the race.

"Slow and steady wins the race" is true for a lot of situations in life. But when it comes to your work-life balance, it's wrong. Dead wrong. Slow and steady doesn't win that race. You know what wins? Work hard. Rest. And then work hard again.

The rabbit had it right. She just rested for too long. But unlike the rabbit, you can set an alarm, a reminder chime. Crush it at work. And then rest. And then crush it again.

So, what does this look like? What are your cycles of stress and rest on an hourly, daily, weekly, monthly, quarterly, and yearly basis?

Hourly Rest

If you work at a job where you sit down and stare at a computer for most of the day, at least once an hour take a quick stretch break. Take sixty seconds to move around a bit. Lightly stretch your body. Give your eyes a break from the screen. A sixty-second stretch break can work wonders for you.

Daily Rest

Take a meal break during your shift. When you work from home, as I do some days, it can be easy to eat lunch in front of your computer. But I want you to get away from your work environment on your lunch break. Change your setting. Get outside if possible. And whatever happens, do not spend your lunch break answering emails. That's not a break. You don't eat a salad with emails. That's like eating a salad with blue cheese. Gross.

As I mentioned earlier, I split my time between working in the corporate world and in the film industry. These two industries treat meal breaks very differently. In the corporate world, you'll probably be rewarded for working through your meal break. In the film industry, you will be punished with a fine if you don't provide your cast and crew with a meal break. Union officials check to make sure everyone has a substantial snack and a meal break. And for good reason. We need to stop placing value on skipping meal breaks and start embracing the truth—we function better at work if we take breaks!

Have you ever walked into a room and noticed it had a particular smell? If you remain in the room for a while, you'll probably stop noticing the smell. Why? Because your brain stops paying careful attention to the same stimulus. Only when you leave the room and then return to it will you notice the smell afresh. There is a term for this: "vigilance decrement." And we can use it to be more effective in our tasks.

In a study from the University of Illinois, two groups performed a task that required significant mental focus. One group performed the task and took breaks. The other group performed the tasks without taking any breaks. Which group do you think got the task done faster? I think you can guess! The group that took breaks completed tasks more quickly and with fewer errors than the group that didn't take any breaks. It may seem counterintuitive, but mental breaks keep you focused. When you deactivate your attention and then reactivate it, your brain returns to the task with a fresh perspective. So, no more salad with emails! Take a break!

Weekly Rest

Some cultures have one day a week during which no one does any work. There is wisdom in that weekly cycle of rest. In the Western world, where the culture supports a 24-7 work week, we have to enforce our own sustainable weekly cycle of work and rest. Can you take at least one day a week when you don't check emails, respond to texts, or do anything at all related to work? If you have been the type of person who is always available, you may need to remind your colleagues that you are unavailable on your day off. Reinforce your boundaries. If you have said you aren't available on Saturdays, don't respond on Saturdays. Stick to your plan.

Maybe one day a week isn't enough for you. If that's the case, I'd like to introduce you to something called... the weekend.

The "weekend" was a concept popular during the twentieth century. It consisted of *two* consecutive days without work. You should try it sometime!

Weekends are an essential part of any discussion of work-life balance. But let's take things a step further. Let's talk about the three-day weekend. Many companies around the world have offered their employees a four-day workweek and haven't found a measurable drop in productivity. Think about that. Employees work 20 percent less hours (this is not a compressed week with more hours on fewer days!) without a loss of productivity. Microsoft Japan famously switched to a three-day weekend and the company experienced a 40 percent boost in productivity. And they aren't alone. According to the Society for Human Resource Management, 60 percent of organizations who tried a four-day workweek experienced higher productivity and increased employee satisfaction. More rest leads to more productivity. That rabbit really was onto something—go hard, rest deep, go hard again.

Perpetual Guardian, a New Zealand–based company, decided to experiment with a four-day workweek. CEO Andrew Barnes introduced something he called the 100:80:100 rule—100 percent pay, 80 percent time, 100 percent productivity. Independent research showed that productivity improved by 25 percent, stress levels dropped by 15 percent, and staff engagement scores improved by 40 percent.

You might not be able to convince your company to switch to a three-day weekend. But you do can set up your own boundaries for work-life balance. And a big part of that is not working outside your regular work hours. Carve out some kind of weekend for yourself. You deserve it!

Yearly Rest

What are some of the soul-nourishing activities you can do each year? What do you do every summer? What do you do every winter break? What does the week after New Year's look like for you? Is there a way you can create yearly rituals that refuel you for the year ahead?

Incorporating rest into your work routine is especially important when working from home. And studies show that remote work, especially during the pandemic, increased stress and anxiety for employees. Just look at these statistics from a study in March 2021. Since Covid began:

- Sixty-four percent of people surveyed said they were working longer hours.
- Thirty-seven percent said their managers expect them to be available on demand.
- Eighty-five percent experienced increased anxiety.

The goal in implementing rest in our lives isn't to avoid stress. The goal is to create a sustainable work life with rhythms of rest built into your hourly, daily, weekly, and yearly routine.

Types of Rest

Dr. Saundra Dalton-Smith is a board-certified physician with over twenty years in clinical practice. She teaches that there are different types of rest we need to thrive in the modern world. They include sensory rest, emotional rest, and mental rest.

Sensory rest: We are bombarded with advertisements, emails, text messages, alerts, chimes, beeps, and buzzes from notifications all through the day. We are, quite simply, overstimulated. It is so helpful to find some quiet time to rest and recharge. When is the last time you put your phone away, turned on some relaxing music, lit some candles, and sat in a comfortable chair? That is a beautiful evening routine. Give your brain a rest from all the stimulation and let yourself relax.

Emotional rest: Whenever you feel like you can't be your authentic self, you are engaging in emotional labor. And emotional labor is exhausting. If you are a flight attendant who must always smile, even when dealing with rude customers, you are engaging in emotional labor. If you work in an environment where you must be bubbly and energetic when you feel quite mellow, you are engaging in emotional labor. This is also why a holiday with your family can leave you depleted!

Anytime you find yourself in a setting that requires you to not be your authentic self, there are two things to remember.

1. Take breaks. This can be your fifteen-minute break at work or it can be slipping away from the family holiday to go for a walk or a workout. You must get away from the people you are performing for and find some time to breathe.

2. Find your people. Who knows you well? Who do you feel comfortable with? Where can you be your authentic self? Maybe you can call a friend or family member and vent to them about what you're going through. Find your people and

No more salad with emails!
Take a break!

connect with them. It'll help you make it through the time you are forced to spend in emotional labor.

Emotional rest can be a way to reward yourself. Every time you smiled at a cranky customer, every time you were patient with that annoying in-law, every time you were polite during a customer service nightmare, you were flexing your emotional muscles. And you deserve a reward! Plan on taking a hot bath or watching an episode of your favorite show or listening to your favorite playlist or getting a massage (or even using a massage gun on yourself). You worked hard, you deserve some rest and relaxation!

Mental rest: Overtaxing your thinking causes decision fatigue. This is why many high performers, such as the prolific author Seth Godin, eat the exact same thing for breakfast every day—it creates one less decision to make! It's why some high-performing tech entrepreneurs wear the exact same outfit every day—one less decision. You may want to vary your diet (a variety of foods contributes to a healthy gut microbiome!) and you may want to change up your clothes (fashion is a fun form of self-expression!). But there are other ways you can preserve your mental energy:

1. Write down your to-do lists. Do you walk around with your to-do list in your mind? That's burning brain cells! A short pencil is better than a long memory. Write down your to-do list on an app on your phone and save your thought life for something more interesting!

2. Create checklists. Anything you must do more than once, such as packing for a business trip or shopping at a specialty grocery store, deserves its own checklist. I started creating checklists for business trips, and they cut my packing time in half! And now I never forget small items like my cell phone charger and snacks for the airplane.

You Can't Separate Work from Life

The term "work-life balance" suggests that your work life and your personal life are separate from each other and can be measured as such. In reality, you bring the same body and brain to both pursuits. Your personal life has a huge impact on your work life and vice versa. If you don't get enough sleep at home, it will affect your cognitive skills at work. If you don't drink enough water at work, you'll bring that dehydration headache home with you. We need to approach this dilemma much more holistically. And for me, that means normalizing self-care in the workplace.

Self-care isn't just something for our personal lives. Self-care should be a regular part of our workplace practices. We should stretch at work. We should take breaks at work. We should go for walks at work. We should socialize and have fun and engage in play at work. We should enjoy fresh air and sunshine at work. The end of a workday should not find us depleted. We should have spent energy—yes! We should engage in rigorous thinking and problem-solving. We may be tired at the end of the workday, but let's not be depleted. This is why leaders need to normalize regular lunch breaks, stretch breaks, going for walks, and connecting socially with coworkers. These activities are essential for a healthy workplace. We must build mentally sustainable work environments.

Companies leading the way with employee wellness are implementing self-care principles in the workplace, providing, for instance:

- Access to fresh air
- Flexible work hours
- Mental health days
- Mental health coverage with health-care plans

- Work-from-home opportunities
- Four-day work weeks

Employees are looking for wellness benefits. One survey found that 60 percent of employees will factor wellness benefits into their job search. And 80 percent of employees between the ages of eighteen and thirty-nine will prioritize wellness benefits in their job selection. The workers entering the workforce now, and in the future, want to work in organizations that prioritize wellness.

Shutdown Ritual

Whether you are working from home or in an office, having a shutdown ritual to transition from your work life to your personal life is important.

Separating work life from your personal life has always been tricky. But it is especially difficult when you work from home. A shutdown ritual can be beneficial in moving from work mode (which, for me, during the pandemic was our kitchen table) to family mode (which was also the kitchen table). How do you transition from work life to family life without changing locations? I shut down all the programs on my laptop, do three minutes of box breathing (see page 11), and change my clothes. Some people find it helpful to pack up their laptop and put it away in a closet or under the bed where it is out of sight. A shutdown ritual might include turning off the overhead lights and turning on smaller lamps around the home. All these things send a signal to your brain that you have shut down the workday and it's time for your personal life. Which leads me to an important point.

The People You're Doing Life With

Busy seasons are part of life. If the people you are doing life with understand when you're having a busy season, they can be prepared for it. Let me tell you a bit about my family...

Susie and I got married in 2003. Susie is an actress and singer who has been in film and TV shows like *Pixels, Beauty and the Beast, A Very Country Christmas, Nikita*, and more. She's also been in dozens of commercials. Currently, she's got a lead role in a theater production that has her at rehearsals five nights a week. She's also a social media manager for a local business. She's busy!

Susie and I have two kids. Our son, Josh, is sixteen years old, eleventh grade, learning to drive, buried in homework, active on his school's basketball team, and has a busy social life and a great laugh. He's awesome.

Our daughter, Ariella, is fifteen years old, ninth grade, also buried in homework, she has been part of a competitive gymnastics team that trains together four times a week, has a busy social life, and is super talented at creative writing! She's amazing.

We are a one-car family. Between rehearsals and basketball games and gymnastics competitions and dentist appointments and school and work and schedules overlapping, our lives are busy! But despite it all, we are genuinely a very close, loving family. And one of the ways we have stayed close, even with four busy schedules, is by having regular family meetings.

Susie and I have family meetings with our kids at least once a month. In these family meetings, we look at a calendar to go through what's on the agenda in the coming weeks. Here are some real-world examples from some of our family meetings:

- Exams are coming up soon. Starting next week, we are cutting back on screen time.

- Mom has a big deadline at the end of the month, so she's not going to be able to drive you around very much. Can you get a ride with friends?
- Dad is away next week, so you have to pack your own lunches for school.
- Summer is coming! Let's decide on some fun family activities.
- Mom and Dad will be on set all day, so if you need anything, here is the person to contact.
- Ari has a gymnastics meet this weekend, so she needs to get a good night's sleep all week. Let's keep the noise down after ten at night.

Always communicate with your loved ones when you are heading into a demanding season. And remember, seasons of stress must be balanced with seasons of rest.

But also…

People without Kids Still Have Lives

Parenting is hard. Everyone knows that. But sometimes parents can make it sound like anyone who isn't a parent isn't busy. Parents can guilt workers who don't have kids into taking more than their fair share of responsibility at work. But people who don't have kids still have lives. You don't deserve to be punished for not being a parent. Everyone gets personal time—kids or no kids.

GET ALL FIRED UP!

Optimize mental wellness: If you don't have the perfect work-life balance, that's totally OK. Remember this equation: Stress + Rest = Blessed.

Ignite joy: Self-care should be a regular part of what we do in the workplace. Give yourself permission to refuel at work—stretch, go for a walk, socialize, or play.

Fuel peak performance: Who else in your life is impacted by your seasons of busy-ness at work? Schedule a monthly family meeting to map out what's ahead and how everyone will be supported.

3
MAKING TIME FOR JOY

We don't stop playing
because we grow old; we grow
old because we stop playing.

GEORGE BERNARD SHAW

ABOUT A year ago, a woman approached me and told me her story. She loves musical theater. In high school, she was in her school musical every year. It was her passion. But after college, she got a good job and settled down in a predictable career. She got married and had two kids. But then, the ache came. She found herself dreaming about the stage. She grew more and more unhappy at work. She longed to be back in the musical theater community. The way she saw it, she had two choices:

1. Quit her job and pursue her dream of being an actress on stage and live happily ever after.

2. Keep her job and forget her dream and live in comfortable misery for the rest of her days.

She asked me to vote for choice number one or choice number two. I voted for choice number three:

3. Keep her job and find a community theater in which to pursue her dream of being an actress on evenings and weekends.

A few months ago this woman wrote me an email, and guess what? After our talk, she looked into community theater and found one only twenty minutes away from her house. They were already in the middle of a production, so she helped sell concessions and made friends with the troupe. Just being around other musical theater people made her come alive. Now they are gearing up for their spring production, and she has a role on stage! She was over the moon with excitement. She said she hasn't been this happy in years.

I know people who played the guitar in a rock band in high school. Now they never touch their guitar. What a shame! Who told these people that if your passion doesn't become a career, you cast it aside?! That's nonsense. You should make time for the things that give you joy! After all, you will be a happier spouse, parent, and coworker if you keep your joy tank full. And that's what this chapter is all about.

My hope is that as you rediscover the magic of play—be it through board games, outdoor adventures, or relaxing hobbies like bird-watching—you will ignite a spark of joy that you carry everywhere you go. Inviting playfulness into your life doesn't detract from your adult responsibilities, it adds a vibrancy that fuels your productivity and zest for life. It's part of being All Fired Up! And to start with, let's talk about laughter.

Laughter

When was the last time you had a belly laugh that left you gasping for breath? Susie and I went to a comedy club with some friends recently, and I laughed so hard that I almost fell out of my chair. It was so good to take a break from all my responsibilities and just let myself laugh.

Laughter is not just an expression of joy, it's also a powerful tool for improving mental health. Studies have shown that laughter reduces stress, anxiety, and depression, and improves overall well-being. In fact, according to a study by the Mayo Clinic, laughter stimulates the release of endorphins, the body's natural feel-good chemicals, which can help relieve pain and promote a sense of relaxation. Laughter can also boost the immune system, lower blood pressure, and improve social connections, all of which can have positive effects on mental health.

One study focused on patients with chronic kidney disease who were undergoing dialysis. Researchers split the patients into two groups—one group watched comedy movies during their treatments while the other group did their regular activities. The patients who were watching comedies during dialysis showed significant improvements in anxiety and depression scores and were less likely to experience complications like hypertension and headache. Another study proved that even the anticipation of laughter lowered stress hormones.

Why am I spending so much time delving into the research on laughter? Kids don't need to read the results of a randomized clinical trial to appreciate the value of a good laugh. But I know some of us adults are so tightly wound that we don't make the time to laugh. And I want to encourage you to make laughter a priority. We need more laughter in our lives and in our relationships.

This year, my wife and I will celebrate our twentieth wedding anniversary. One of the ways we stay connected to each other is through laughter. Susie will text me in the middle of the day when we are both at home! I'll check my message and see some funny meme about penguins in Antarctica or a hilarious video of a panda bear rolling down a hill. We sit and watch funny movies and TV shows and just laugh together. It's an important part of our relationship, and I'm convinced it's one of the reasons we still enjoy each other's company. Even the best relationships go through difficult seasons. Laughter can be the glue that holds a strained relationship together. I've seen it work with parents and their teens. I've seen it work on social media when politics have divided siblings. I've seen it work between in-laws. Laughter is like the oil that keeps an engine running smoothly. But of course, laughter isn't the only source of joy.

Active Joy

I have a theory. People who spend twenty minutes a day in *active joy* will be happier throughout the day and more resilient in tough times. Notice I said *active* joy. Reading is great for your mental health but even if you are reading your favorite novel, it isn't active. And that's fine—rest and relaxation are crucial for a healthy work-life balance too. But when I'm talking about *joy* I'm talking about *action*. I want you to spend twenty minutes a day, every day, *doing something active* that brings you joy.

How to find active joy in three easy steps:
1. Put on a pair of headphones.
2. Find one of your favorite songs from when you were a teenager.
3. Dance wildly.

Dancing is one of the best ways to connect with your body. Many Indigenous cultures throughout the world use dance as a form of sacred movement. Some West African cultures dance at funeral services to process their grief. Think about that. In their saddest moment, they dance to music. They understand grief must be processed, not only in the mind but in the body. Still today in New Orleans, dancing is part of many funeral services.

Dance is not just a form of entertainment or artistic expression, it's also a means of achieving catharsis. It is a way of releasing pent-up emotions, connecting with the community, and seeking spiritual renewal. Whether it is the traditional dances of the Māori, the powwows of Native American tribes, or the ritual dances of the Ainu people in Japan, dance can involve the use of music and song to create a sense of unity and release. Through dance, people express their deepest emotions, heal their trauma, and celebrate their identity. But in Western culture, it's often different...

When I'm speaking at a convention in Winnipeg or a corporate event in Orlando and I encourage people to dance, a funny thing happens. They think I'm talking about nightclubs and valet parking and bottle service. When people hear the word "dance," they think they need to shave their legs and book a babysitter. Some people think dancing isn't an option for them because they don't have a natural sense of rhythm, or someone told them that they aren't a "good" dancer. But as the African proverb says, "If you can talk, you can sing; and if you can walk, you can dance!"

Picture a bunch of three-year-olds dancing in preschool. That's the kind of dancing I'm talking about. Those three-year-olds aren't trying to be cool. They aren't trying to impress anyone. They aren't worried about having rhythm. They are just enjoying their bodies moving to music. Dancing is the ultimate catharsis. Do not let nightclub culture rob you of the joy of movement!

I don't know you very well, but I think music and dancing should play a much bigger role in your life. Unless you are a professional dancer and you dance all day long and you just need some silence in your life—that is totally understandable. But for everyone else: I don't think you dance enough. I don't think you "wild out" enough. And even those of you who hit the club every couple of months and dance yourselves sweaty—that's not enough. You don't need a nightclub to enjoy loud music—your bedroom will do just fine. You don't need a DJ to provide the right tunes—your playlist will do just fine. You don't need huge speakers—your headphones will do just fine. And you don't need to wait for Saturday night—Monday afternoon works too.

The problem with dancing only when you are at a wedding or a nightclub is that you are missing out on a chance for joy in your daily life. I want you to make a habit of putting on some headphones, closing the blinds in your bedroom, and dancing your heart out to one song. I'm talking three minutes. That can be part of your daily routine. And please, for the love of all that is sacred, don't try to dance well. I want you to dance silly. I want you to dance sloppy. I want you to dance like an octopus on roller skates. The goal of this is *active joy*, not coordination.

The Wild Accountant

I worked with an accountant in Toronto who had an amazing work-life balance. At work, he was organized, punctual, and reliable. He could crunch numbers with the best of them. He was a good, dependable accountant. But on weekends he turned into a motorcycle-riding, cliff-diving, barefoot-water-skiing adrenaline junkie. In the summers, he had water-skiing competitions with his teenage sons; and in the winters, he played ice hockey on frozen ponds. At work, he was all business. And on weekends, he was all kinds of wild. That's the type of work-life balance I admire.

I dare you to try it. I dare you to add twenty minutes of active joy to your day. Twenty minutes of dancing. Twenty minutes on a trampoline. Twenty minutes of singing karaoke. Twenty minutes of improv games with an online drama club. Twenty minutes of your favorite sport. Twenty minutes of active joy. Every day. You deserve it!

Maple Syrup

I'm a Canadian. We make the best maple syrup on earth. (I know some folks in Vermont will clap back at that statement, but it's true.) If you've never been to a maple syrup festival, I encourage you to add it to your bucket list. Maple sap flows up the trees in early spring, and you can put a "tap" into the trunk of the trees to catch the sap in a bucket. The sap is then boiled down to the perfection known as 100 percent pure maple syrup.

For the love of all that is sacred, dance silly. Dance sloppy. Dance like an octopus on roller skates. **The goal of this is *active joy*.**

Canadians are known for being polite. But if you offer a Canadian some pancakes with fake syrup, you'll see we also have a mean streak. My family and I have actually traveled with real maple syrup in the car so we can use the good stuff when we're eating hotel breakfasts. You can't beat the taste of real maple syrup. I dare say it's one of the most joy-inspiring foods on the planet. But that's not why I'm including it in a chapter about joy. I'm including it because the only way to get that maple syrup is to tap into the tree. And there is a source of joy available to you twenty-four hours a day, if you just tap into it... and that, my dear reader, is gratitude!

The Power of Gratitude

Did you know that gratitude unlocks joy? It's true. Hundreds of studies have proven it over and over again. People who intentionally practice gratitude are happier, more optimistic, and have a greater sense of fulfillment compared with those who don't practice gratitude. Notice the key difference here is the word "practice." We're not talking about people who are naturally positive or grateful. We're talking about people who adopted a practice of gratitude. For some, that means writing ten things they are thankful for in a gratitude journal. For others, it means writing a heartfelt letter of thanks to a person in their lives. And for others, it means ten minutes of silence, thinking about all the things they are grateful for in their lives. Gratitude is not a disposition, it is a practice. And one that produces incredible rewards!

The benefits of a gratitude practice are amazing: better health, more restful sleep, higher rates of happiness and life satisfaction, increased energy levels, lower levels of depressive symptoms, reduced anxiety, and more. But these benefits are unlocked through practice—not knowledge. So, what are we waiting for? Let's get these benefits!

Three enjoyable ways to be actively grateful:
1 Write a letter of gratitude to someone who made a difference in your life and share it with them!
2 Write a list of twenty things you are thankful for in your life.
3 Find a quiet place where you can relax. Set a ten-minute timer and spend ten minutes thinking about all the things in your life you are thankful for.

The Importance of Play

We've all heard the expression "all work and no play makes Jack a dull boy." But author Joline Godfrey took it a step further by pointing out, "All work and no play doesn't just make Jill and Jack dull; it kills the potential of discovery, mastery, and openness to change and flexibility and hinders innovation and invention." Like laughter, play is not just for kids—it is an essential part of our mental health and well-being, regardless of our age. From board games to team sports, from puzzles to creative hobbies, play provides heaps of benefits for the brain and body. Some studies suggest that the more you engage in play, the more innovative and productive you'll be at work.

Play has been shown to improve cognitive function, creativity, and problem-solving skills. For example, the use of improv games in corporate training has become increasingly popular in recent years because it helps leaders develop skills such as active listening, adaptability, and collaboration. By engaging in playful activities that encourage spontaneity, we can tap into our natural creativity and become more agile and resilient in the face of challenges.

Play is an important part of building social connections as well. Play can foster a sense of community, bringing people together in ways that promote bonding and emotional well-being. During a time when many of us spend a significant amount of our day isolated and disconnected from others, play is a fun way to build relationships and enhance a sense of belonging.

Adding a bit of adventure to your everyday routines is another form of play. Have you ever tried geocaching? It's a real-world outdoor treasure hunting game using GPS-enabled devices. It's about not just the thrill of the hunt but also the joy of exploring new surroundings, both in your local area and where your travels take you. I had never tried it until my stepbrother Vincent brought our whole family on a geocache treasure hunt right in our neighborhood. It was a blast!

Sometimes "play" can be very quiet and calm. If you love nature, bird-watching can be a delightful hobby that also serves as a playful activity. The thrill of spotting and identifying a rare species can bring a jolt of joy unlike any other. My aunt Cathy and uncle Chris love bird-watching, and it gives them something to look forward to whenever they travel to a new part of the world.

In the digital world, online multiplayer games have become a popular form of play, fostering teamwork and camaraderie between players across the globe. These are not just about winning the game. They are also about connecting with people and the excitement of a shared mission. You are never too old for video games! Ask some friends or family members if they can show you some games you might enjoy. I'm not a huge gamer, but I loved playing the game *Inside* by Danish video game developer Playdead. This puzzle game really gets you thinking!

Speaking of games that get you thinking, I love playing chess. The online chess world is thriving right now. If you used to play when you were younger, give online chess a try!

Maybe you could join a science-fiction book club. Or perhaps you would enjoy an escape room with friends. Maybe you should schedule a games night once a week. I wonder if you need to rediscover your love for movies? If your life is weighed down with responsibilities, I'm here to remind you that you need a spark of joy to keep your engine running!

GET ALL FIRED UP!

Optimize mental wellness: Every time you make time for joy, you're adding fuel to your tank. Try scheduling twenty minutes of joyful activity into your day, just like you might make time in your calendar for a workout or a coffee date.

Ignite joy: Dance! Just dance!

Fuel peak performance: Incorporate playtime activities (community theater, games night, geocaching, bird-watching, escape rooms, video games) to fuel creativity and innovation.

HOW TO HANDLE HARD DAYS

Today was a total waste of makeup.

UNKNOWN

I'VE WORKED WITH successful actors, all-star athletes, and Fortune 500 executives. They have one thing in common: all of them go through tough times. They all have mornings they don't want to get out of bed. They all get the blahs. They all have afternoons when they feel miserable. They all make wrong decisions from time to time. Every single one.

But there is another thing the high performers I've worked with have in common—they move past failure. They shake it off and take the next step. They learn from their shortcomings and apply that wisdom to their next challenge. And that is something all of us can learn to do.

The truth is, sometimes the day-to-day grind is tough. From keeping up with emails, making time for your family, exercising, putting together materials for that client, taking the dog for two walks, reading those business development books, keeping the romance alive with your partner and remembering to call your mom and registering to vote and renewing the sticker on your license plate at the DMV... life is a challenge! The question is not, Will you have hard days? The question is, What will you do when you're having a hard day? And that's the subject of this chapter.

What Happens When You're in a Funk?

My friends would describe me as a happy person. My wife and kids would say the same. I'm good-natured, optimistic, and cheerful. But sometimes I feel down in the dumps. Sometimes I feel anxious and irritable. Other times I feel lethargic and numb. And the million-dollar question is... How do you break out of a funk and get back to a place where you are operating smoothly?

When you are operating smoothly, you can put up with frustrations. If your toddler spills their cereal on the kitchen floor, it's no big deal—you can clean it up together. If the barista gets your order wrong, it doesn't faze you—you crack a joke as you hand the drink back and ask for a new one. If there's more traffic than usual, you don't sweat it—that's more time to listen to your favorite podcast. When you are operating smoothly, you are a joy to be around.

Unfortunately, if you are human, you don't spend all day, every day, in your sweet spot. Even high performers find themselves in a funk. And this is a big deal. When you're in a negative headspace, you won't be effective at work, you won't be helpful to your friends, and your parenting skills will stink. So, learning how to get out of a funk is crucial. For me, there are two types of funks that get me into trouble, and I'd venture you experience something like them too. I call them "overheated" and "out of gas."

Broadly speaking, when the nervous system gets overwhelmed, it responds in two distinct ways. Dr. Daniel Siegel, a clinical professor at UCLA, refers to these states as "hyperarousal" and "hypoarousal." You might not be familiar with these terms, but I'm willing to bet you're familiar with the feelings.

Hyperarousal (or overheated) speaks to feeling overstressed and anxious. When I am overheated, my thoughts are overwhelming, my heart rate is increased, and I feel stressed out. Hypoarousal (out of gas) speaks to feeling unmotivated and lethargic. When I am out of gas, I feel numb. I feel cynical about the future, sluggish, helpless, and hopeless. I'm tired and worn out emotionally.

I think of "overheated" and "out of gas" as existing on opposite ends of a spectrum, with a sweet spot in the middle: operating smoothly.

Operating Smoothly
calm, resilient, balanced,
"I got this!", creative, thoughtful,
rational, engaged, thriving

Out of Gas
numb, lethargic, sad,
not enough stimulation,
sluggish, "who cares?",
languishing, unmotivated

Overheated
overwhelmed, irritable,
too much stimulation,
racing thoughts, edgy,
jumpy, anxious, angry

Driving Stick Shift

When I was seventeen, my brother taught me how to drive a manual transmission car. They're still common in many parts of the world, but in North America, most people don't know how to drive a stick shift. You see, most cars have an automatic transmission, where the engine automatically shifts between gears as the car's speed increases. But with manual transmission, the driver manually shifts between gears. When you are driving very slowly, you are in first gear. As you get a little faster, you start to hear the engine straining and you shift to second gear. As you get even faster, you hear the engine straining again, and you shift to third. If you need to slow down, you don't always need to pump the brakes, sometimes you can downshift.

When it comes to our nervous systems, most of us are operating on automatic. We are unaware of the shifts happening within our bodies as we move from feeling confident and in control to feeling overwhelmed and anxious, to feeling burnt out and helpless. The good news is, when we are aware of our inner states, we can learn how to manually shift ourselves back to our sweet spot—where we're operating smoothly.

With manual transmission, the sound of the engine straining is one indication that you need to shift gears. What about your nervous system? How does your nervous system tell you that you might need a shift?

I've come to recognize the signs when I'm overheated or out of gas. If my heart rate is elevated and my hands are sweaty, I'm overheated. If I'm irritable, and restless, and I feel like I might explode, I'm overheated. I need to do some activities to return to my sweet spot.

On the other hand, if I'm feeling lazy and tired and unfocused and I can't even tell if I'm hungry and the thought of even walking across the room to get my water bottle seems overwhelming... I'm out of gas. It's time for some shifting to get myself operating smoothly.

Paying attention to what is happening within your body is key to knowing how to navigate your way back to your sweet spot.

Look at the graphic on page 51 again. Remember, operating smoothly is the objective. If you're overheated, you need to come down to get back to your sweet spot. You need to do activities that are grounding and relaxing. You need to slow your pace. You need to pause. To use the manual transmission analogy, you need to *downshift*.

If you're out of gas, you need to do activities that are stimulating. You need some energy and excitement. You need to move. Again, to use the manual transmission analogy, you need to *upshift*.

So, on a bad day, when you find yourself feeling stressed out, anxious, and irritable, I want you to try some of these *downshifting* activities:

- Meditate (see pages 8-15).
- Practice mindfulness.
- Take a nap.
- Write in a journal.
- Sketch or use a coloring book.
- Play an instrument.
- Listen to relaxing music.
- Do breathwork focused on the exhale (see page 84).

Remember: breathe out to mellow out. Or if you want to feel stimulated, reverse it: focus on a longer, more forceful inhale.

Or if you find yourself feeling sluggish and unmotivated, try some *upshifting* activities:

- Go for a walk.
- Clean your space.
- Look at your vision board.
- Dance to your favorite song.
- Tackle tiny items on your to-do list.
- Shower and get dressed.
- Listen to upbeat music.
- Do breathwork focused on the inhale (see page 58).

Sometimes you find yourself in a negative headspace and you don't know if you need to downshift or upshift—you just know you need to break out of that funk! I've been there too. So if you're having a bad day and you don't know what to do, try one of these activities.

High-Intensity Workout

Doing a high-intensity workout fundamentally changes your state. It's one of the best ways to break out of a funk. And the science explains why.

Moving your body stimulates your happy hormones like serotonin. That's why you feel so great after a workout. Sometimes I'll do a workout not for the physical benefits but for the mood boost and creative ideas that follow a flood of serotonin.

And exercise isn't just good for creative thinking, studies suggest that it may help with depressive symptoms as well. One study showed that intense exercise boosts the levels of two neurotransmitters in the brain, glutamate and GABA, which are depleted in people suffering with depression. Another study showed that intense exercise can alter your brain by increasing a protein called BDNF, which regulates brain function and mood. Low levels of BDNF are linked with depression, bipolar disorder, and schizophrenia.

You probably already know a workout will help when you're feeling off. But if you're like me, the last thing you want to do when you're feeling down is go for a jog. Sometimes when I lack the motivation to do a full workout, I just need to take the first step toward one. Here's how it works for me...

When I'm on the couch, I don't want to go for a workout, but I can talk myself into standing up and stretching.

Once I'm standing up and stretching, I can talk myself into a walk around the block.

Once I walk around the block, I can talk myself into running around the block.

Once I run around the block, I can talk myself into doing a few push-ups and a thirty-second plank. Soon enough, my muscles are burning, I'm out of breath, and I just finished a high-intensity workout. And my brain is reaping all the benefits!

Speaking of benefits, another thing you should try is...

Cold Showers

I never step into a cold shower—it's too much of a shock to my system. So, I start with a warm shower and, every thirty seconds or so, I get the water a little bit cooler and let my body adjust to that new temperature. The cooler water is awful for the first ten seconds or so, but then I adjust. The water gets cooler and cooler until I'm at the coldest setting. And then I try to stay in that cold water for two or three minutes. And when I turn the water off? I feel amazing! I am alert, energized, and refocused. It works every time! Here's why.

Cold showers stimulate your sympathetic nervous system. That's the part of your body responsible for your fight-or-flight response. (We'll go a little deeper with this in chapter 6.) A cold shower gives you a rush of endorphins (more happy chemicals) and a shot of adrenaline. It's a mood-boosting, energy-inducing, elated-chemical rush to the head. It's a little discomfort that comes with a lot of benefits. Give it a try!

Connect with a Friend

One of the best things you can do for your mental health is to connect with another person. This can be a deep conversation with a good friend or even a short chat with the barista at your coffee shop. The Stanford University School of Medicine released a study proving that oxytocin—nicknamed the "love hormone" because of its role in mother-child bonding as well as sexual attachments—is involved in a wide range of social interactions. The researchers found that oxytocin released through any social connectivity, from a friendly chat with a neighbor to bonding with a fellow sports fan over a recent win to having coffee with a lifelong friend, triggers a release of serotonin. In a chain reaction, serotonin activates the reward system in the brain, which results in feelings of happiness and contentment. To put it simply: social connections are good for your mental health!

Breathwork

I mentioned breathwork in the lists of downshifting and upshifting activities, but it really deserves a more rigorous explanation. I'll be honest: the first time someone told me to practice breathing, I almost laughed. I'm so good at breathing, I do it in my sleep. What is there to practice?! I've since learned the science behind intentional breathwork. It is incredibly effective at reducing anxiety, alleviating tension, helping with insomnia, and boosting focus. Here's how it works.

Different patterns of breathing are associated with different emotions. For example, when you are stressed out and anxious, your breathing will be fast, shallow, and irregular. But when you feel peaceful and safe, your breathing will be slow, deep, and regular. So, when you follow breathing patterns associated with certain emotions, you can actually begin to feel those emotions!

When you inhale, it speeds up your heart rate. When you exhale, it slows down your heart rate. So, if you want to slow down your heart rate and feel calmer, try breathing techniques that focus on a longer, more forceful exhale. Remember: breathe out to mellow out. Or if you want to feel stimulated, reverse it: try breathing techniques that focus on a longer, more forceful inhale. Breathing intentionally like this can trigger your nervous system and get you heading in the right direction.

The Four-Seven-Eight Breathing Exercise

For a breathing exercise that helps you relax, I highly recommend the four-seven-eight breathing exercise. It is a type of yogic breathing that I learned about from Dr. Andrew Weil, the founder and director of the Center for Integrative Medicine at the University of Arizona. It is super easy to learn and lasts for only thirty seconds. And, wow, what a difference it makes! Here's how it works: First, put the tip of your tongue against the ridge of flesh just behind your upper front teeth. Make a *whoosh* sound as you exhale fully through your mouth. Then, follow this breathing pattern:

- Inhale quietly through your nose for a count of four.
- Hold your breath for a count of seven.
- Exhale audibly through your mouth for a count of eight.

That completes one breath cycle. Repeat the process three more times, for a total of four cycles. Remember, you always inhale quietly through your nose and exhale audibly through your mouth. Your tongue remains in place, and your exhale takes twice as long as your inhale. That's key. Focus on the ratio of four-seven-eight. When I first heard about four-seven-eight breathing I thought it was supposed to be four *seconds* followed by seven seconds followed by eight seconds. But that's not it. Dr. Weil completes four cycles in about thirty seconds. So set your own rhythm, count to four as you inhale through your nose, count to seven as you hold your breath, count to eight as you exhale through your mouth. As long as you keep the same pace for each count, you're doing it right.

By stimulating your vagus nerve, this breathing exercise acts like a natural tranquilizer for your nervous system. And the results get more powerful the more you practice it. Dr. Weil recommends doing four-seven-eight breathing at least twice a day. Why not give it a try? It only takes about thirty seconds. The next time you feel tense or under pressure, try four rounds of four-seven-eight breathing before you react.

GET ALL FIRED UP!

Optimize mental wellness: If you're like me, you're human and you're going to get into a funk now and then. Start to pay attention to what kind of funk you're in and what you need to do about it. Do you need to downshift or upshift?

Ignite joy: Do a high-intensity workout. You won't regret it.

Fuel peak performance: Whatever the reason for your funk, you can learn to shake it off. Search for self-acceptance. Even the highest achievers have their off days.

5

THE POWER OF SELF-AWARENESS

The privilege of a lifetime is to become who you truly are.

CARL JUNG

WAS AWAY for a one-week leadership training program in British Columbia. If you've never been to Canada's West Coast, add it to your bucket list. The mountains, the oceans, the trees... BC in the summertime is heaven on earth. In the wintertime, BC is more like ocean on earth... it's rainy. But this was summertime, and I was in my element. I would be eating great food and learning great content about being a great leader. It really was great.

Until it wasn't. On day three, in the middle of a morning session on time management, I began to feel hot. But the room wasn't warm. I felt claustrophobic, even though I had lots of space around me. Something was just wrong. I couldn't focus. I felt like the walls were closing in on me. It was very unnerving.

I made it through the session and enjoyed lunch with my colleagues. After lunch, we had free time and I played basketball with a few of the leaders. But through it all, I had this nagging feeling in the back of my mind: something was off.

That night I stayed up late trading leadership stories with my roommate. I woke up the next morning, had an early breakfast with my cohort, and settled in to the morning session, listening to a leader speak about courage and vulnerability, one of my favorite subjects. This was going to be good.

Only it wasn't. It happened again—the walls started closing in on me. I couldn't concentrate. I felt jumpy. I couldn't put my finger on what was bothering me. Too much coffee? Not enough sleep? Was something about the content rubbing me the wrong way?

I was so bothered that after lunch, rather than playing basketball with the others, I decided to go for a walk by myself to figure out what was going on with me. I walked up a trail and took in the scenery: the mountains, the ocean, the trees, the birds... it was beautiful. I walked for about twenty minutes and stopped at a clearing.

I breathed in the fresh air.

I watched the birds overhead.

I listened to the sound of the wind in the trees.

It was quiet. It was peaceful. And... I realized this was my first time alone in four days. From the time I woke up until the time I went to sleep, I had been surrounded by people. And the people were great, but they were still... people.

Part of my routine at home always involves some time alone. Sometimes I go for a run by myself; sometimes I have a thirty-minute drive home alone in the car. But every day, I always have some time to myself. And it was alone in the mountains of BC that I discovered a major key to my overall well-being: I *need* this time to myself every day to recharge. I love being around people. I feel my tank refilling when I'm around people having a good conversation. But it turns out that I have two tanks that need to be filled. One requires people. One requires alone time. And if I don't get some alone time every day, I start to malfunction. So, for the rest of that week in BC, I intentionally set aside thirty minutes a day for alone time. And that made all the difference. I could enjoy the sessions, and the company of other leaders, because I was taking time to recharge.

Self-awareness includes knowing what you need to be at your best and then having the discipline to put those things into practice. But it all starts with knowledge of self. What fuels you? What drains you? What day in the coming week might be especially hard for you? What will you do to recharge your battery when the day is done? This is all part of self-awareness. And self-awareness is a key indicator for successful leaders.

Self-Awareness for Leaders

The Stanford Graduate School of Business wanted to determine the most important capability for business leaders to develop. Is it communication skills? Decision-making? Adaptability? While these are all important, the results of their survey were a surprise to many people. They found that self-awareness was the number one most important skill for business leaders to develop. Leaders need to know their strengths and weaknesses to leverage them or compensate for them.

Another study, this one of 486 publicly traded companies, proved that self-awareness impacts stock performance. Employees of companies with strong financial performance were found to have higher levels of self-awareness than employees of poorly performing companies. Self-awareness is good for the bottom line!

On a personal level, knowing yourself well may be the first step in living a fulfilling life. When you are clear on your values and beliefs, you can make choices that bring you joy, rather than simply following what others think is best for you. There is peace of mind when you know you haven't violated your true self just to fit in with the crowd. As the French proverb says, "There is no pillow so soft as a clear conscience."

So, what do I mean when I say "self-awareness"? What are some of the areas we can learn to grow in self-knowledge?

Strengths and Weaknesses

A big part of self-awareness is being honest with yourself about your strengths and weaknesses. If you don't know what your strengths are, you won't be able to contribute meaningfully to your projects. Some people were raised to be so humble that they can't acknowledge that they even have any strengths! This is a huge mistake. Every single person has gifts and talents. And guess what? We need your gifts and talents! We need you to shine! And that starts with an awareness of your strengths and a will to sharpen those skills even more.

On the other end of the spectrum are people who aren't aware of their weaknesses. Some people are overly confident in areas where they don't have expertise. That is a recipe for disaster. Everyone has weak points—knowing where yours are, and using people and resources to mitigate them, is wise. In short, self-awareness involves knowing your strengths to leverage them and knowing your weaknesses to address them.

Managing Emotions

Self-awareness also allows you to manage your emotions, making you more adaptable in difficult situations. When you recognize your triggers, you can take steps to regulate your emotions and respond appropriately. And when you can be calm under pressure, people trust you more.

On the flip side, if you don't recognize your triggers, you may overreact to situations without being aware of it. This can have a negative impact on job performance and personal relationships. When you are unaware of how you are responding to stressful situations, it can lead to communication breakdowns, conflicts with colleagues, and damaged personal and professional relationships. Remember, self-awareness is not about being perfect or having all the answers. It's about being honest with yourself and committed to improvement. And give yourself heaps and heaps of self-compassion on the journey! Everyone is a work in progress. Be kind to yourself as you continue to learn and grow.

Hopefully, by now I've convinced you of the importance of self-awareness. But now the question is, How do you become more self-aware? One way is to find a good mentor.

Self-awareness includes knowing what you need to be at your best and then having the discipline to put those things into practice.

Mentors

Often, we are too close to ourselves to see our strengths and weaknesses objectively. A mentor can offer an outside perspective and honest feedback about what they see. For example, a mentor might recognize that you have excellent communication skills and encourage you to seek out more public speaking opportunities. And just as you are gaining confidence in that area, your mentor can point out a weakness in your time management skills and help you develop strategies to improve. To adapt a quote from Benjamin Franklin, the school of experience is for the fool; mentorship is for the wise.

A good mentor is a great way to discover your own strengths and weaknesses. Isn't it interesting that we need others to know ourselves? Of course, there are other ways to develop self-awareness, and I want to share the best tool I have found when it comes to knowing yourself on a deeper level. It's called the Enneagram.

The Enneagram

The Enneagram is a personality typing system that has been around for hundreds of years. It teaches that there are nine different personality types, and when we're little, we choose a style that helps us navigate our way in the world. Here's the game-changer, though: each personality type has an unconscious drive that affects behavior, motivation, feelings, and thoughts.

1. **The Reformer:** who has a strong sense of right and wrong and feels compelled to make the world a better place
2. **The Helper:** who needs to be needed and to be appreciated for helping others

3. **The Achiever:** who has a strong inner drive to succeed and be admired

4. **The Individualist:** who needs to feel special and unique but also often feels misunderstood

5. **The Investigator:** who needs to know and understand situations and will stand back to observe the world around them

6. **The Loyalist:** who looks for security and stability, seeks guidance from authority, and may feel anxious

7. **The Enthusiast:** who needs adventure and excitement and seeks out new experiences, but doesn't necessarily stick with things

8. **The Challenger:** who likes control and power, needs to protect themselves and others, and may seem confrontational

9. **The Peacemaker:** who needs peace and harmony and may avoid conflict or may struggle with self-assertion

When you know your personality type, and the unconscious drive that accompanies it, you can keep yourself out of all kinds of trouble. But if you aren't aware of what drives you at an unconscious level, you'll find yourself repeating self-defeating patterns throughout your life with no understanding of why these things are happening.

I want you to get curious about which of the nine personality types you are, as knowing your type can be a real game-changer. There are lots of online tests to find your type. I took the test on the Truity website. It cost twenty dollars and was super effective for me. But there are free tests online as well. Other people prefer to learn about all nine types rather than taking a test online. Whatever your approach, I highly encourage you to lean into the Enneagram.

Knowing How Your Engine Works

Let me take a moment to explain how knowing my type has helped me so much. I'm a type 3 on the Enneagram, the Achiever. I'm driven by a need to appear successful. I'm driven by a desire to be admired. I'm driven by productivity and achievement. When I first read a description of my type, I was appalled. It was embarrassing. But it also helped me recognize the engine that was driving a lot of my behavior. I think that's a good way to think about personality—it's an internal engine that is driving our behavior. Here's how my engine works.

When I walk into a social event, I have an overwhelming desire to impress people. I was never consciously aware of it, but that was the engine running in the background. I would take the temperature of the room to try to get a sense of who I need to be to be impressive in this environment. Then I would turn up the volume on some parts of my personality and turn it down on others to really shine. I found myself lying about my opinion to fit in. I found myself exaggerating to the point of lying just to be impressive. Whenever I fall into that awful pattern of changing who I am to impress others, I always walk away feeling nauseous.

I didn't know I was trying to be impressive. I would find myself walking away from an interaction with someone, wondering why I just lied or why I just pretended I hated some movie that I loved or why I just exaggerated about something totally irrelevant. I wasn't being true to myself, and I didn't know what type of situation would make me repeat the behavior again. Reading about my Enneagram type was a painful, but helpful, insight.

I realized that the engine driving my behavior was a personality type I gravitated to as a child. I probably wasn't getting all the attention I craved, and somewhere along the way, I must have figured out that if I can be impressive, I will get attention and love. Ian Morgan Cron, a well-respected expert in the Enneagram, says that if you aren't aware of the survival skills you adopted in childhood, you will live your adult years with an operation manual written by a child. As Carl Jung said, "Until you make the unconscious conscious, it will direct your life and you will call it fate." And that's exactly what I was doing. I was trying to do anything I could to impress people so that I would earn their attention and love. And often I was missing out on a genuine connection while looking for admiration.

One of my favorite movies of all time is *Birdman* by Alejandro González Iñárritu. In the film, one character warns another about the dangers of confusing admiration for love. That's exactly what I was doing. I was missing out on genuine, meaningful connections by trying to impress people with my personality or my accomplishments or my refined opinion on twentieth-century literature.

That's why the Enneagram has been such a gift to me. I can look at myself with self-compassion, understand why I chose this behavior as a child, and choose different behaviors going forward. And now, before I walk into any social event, I put my hand on my chest and say to myself: "Anthony, you don't need to impress anyone. Just be yourself."

Can I tell you something amazing? I have so much more fun at events now that I'm not trying to impress anyone. Trying to be impressive is exhausting. I heard a woman complain about her husband by saying, "Going anywhere with you is exhausting! It's like you're campaigning to be the mayor of nothing." He must have been a type 3!

I hope you'll consider learning more about the Enneagram. It is the most powerful self-awareness tool I have ever used. It has helped me professionally and personally. I wonder what you could learn about yourself by diving deeper into your own Enneagram type. Give it a try!

GET ALL FIRED UP!

Optimize mental wellness: A big key to mental health is being aware of what you need in any given moment and resourcing yourself accordingly. This can happen through self-awareness. Pay attention to what fills your tank, and give yourself what you need to thrive!

Ignite joy: Where do you shine? Identify one of the strengths you bring to a project.

Fuel peak performance: Use the resources available to you to build your self-knowledge, including understanding your weaknesses. The Enneagram is a great tool for this. When you know your weaknesses, you can shore yourself up accordingly.

6

DEALING WITH ANXIETY

The strongest people are not those who show strength in front of the world, but those who fight and win battles that others do not know anything about.

JONATHAN HARNISCH

O**NE NIGHT,** as I was sound asleep, a noise jolted me awake. It sounded like someone was trying to break in through my window. My heart started racing, and I felt fear wash over me. My stomach twisted in knots. Legs shaking, I got out of bed and slowly approached the window. I was terrified.

But as I reached the window, I realized that the noise was not an intruder—it was just the sound of an icy storm battering the glass. I felt instant relief. The knot in my stomach untangled, the shivers stopped, and the tension in my throat released. Within just a few minutes, I had gone from complete peace to utter fear and back to complete peace once again.

When there is a clear and present danger, your body initiates a fear response—all systems are on high alert. And, in usual circumstances, if you realize there is no danger, the fear subsides and your body relaxes.

With anxiety, your body initiates that same fear response—all systems on high alert—even when there is no clear, identifiable threat. The fear lingers without an end in sight. It feels awful. And for me, it can last for days or even weeks.

When I am really under the waves of anxiety, the simplest task feels overwhelming. Writing an email feels like climbing a mountain. Paying a parking ticket feels like running a marathon. Everything is harder when I am feeling anxious. Maybe you can relate?

Anxiety Soundtrack

My anxiety is like a soundtrack that plays throughout my entire day. You know in a scary movie when the monster isn't on screen yet, but that terrifying music starts playing in the background and you know something bad is coming? Yeah. That's what my anxiety soundtrack sounds like. Those deep bass notes of impending doom rumble in my soul. It's awful. Sometimes this noise is on repeat all day. Whether I'm working or eating or helping my kids with their homework, the awful anxiety soundtrack just hums away in the background. Sometimes the soundtrack gets so loud that it's hard to concentrate on anything else. Other times, it's just a constant looming presence.

If there were lyrics to my soundtrack, it would probably sound something like this:

You aren't safe.
You'll never be safe.
Something bad is coming.

Those aren't great lyrics. They don't even rhyme. But they sure strike fear in my nervous system. I have tried so many ways of dealing with anxiety. I'm going to share the most helpful things I've learned here. My hope is that if you suffer from anxiety, some of these coping strategies may bring you some relief. But I want you to remember, what works for one doesn't always work for all. If you try these methods and you don't find them helpful, don't be discouraged. You aren't alone.

Lots of high achievers struggle with anxiety. We are driven. We are ambitious. We've got a great work ethic. Those are good qualities. But there's a flip side. We tend to overwork. We struggle with work-life balance. And we're prone to anxiety. And since people know us as high performers, we often choose to hide our anxiety. We are like a duck—calm and collected above the surface but paddling like mad in the water. It's time to get honest about the anxiety we feel.

With that said, let's look at what anxiety is and how to deal with it effectively.

What Is Anxiety?

To understand anxiety, it helps to know some basics about the nervous system, because it plays a huge role in all those heart-racing, hand-sweating, shallow-breathing feelings.

I'm going to get a little scientific here, but please don't skip this part. This won't be a boring high school biology class. This will give you some information about how to get off the anxiety train! Very simply put, two branches of the nervous system play a role in responding to stress.

The sympathetic nervous system (SNS) is responsible for the body's fight-or-flight response. When the SNS is activated, it releases stress hormones like adrenaline and cortisol. These hormones increase heart rate, blood pressure, and sugar levels in the blood, preparing the body to respond to an emergency. Fight-or-flight mode is supposed to be a *short-term response* to an immediate threat.

The parasympathetic nervous system (PNS) is responsible for the body's relaxation response. It counterbalances the effects of the SNS and promotes feelings of calm and well-being. When the PNS is activated, it releases acetylcholine, which slows heart rate, lowers blood pressure, and relaxes the muscles. When you are functioning optimally, an immediate threat triggers the fight-or-flight response (SNS) and your body goes on high alert; and once the threat is gone, the relaxation response (PNS) is activated, and you calm down. The body was designed to fluctuate between these two responses.

The trouble so many of us are dealing with is an overactive fight-or-flight response. Our SNS is constantly on high alert, and we feel overwhelmed and on the verge of burnout. Prolonged activation of the fight-or-flight response can lead to chronic stress, which is associated with conditions like anxiety and depression.

I want to be clear that the fight-or-flight response is not an inherently bad thing. In fact, it can keep you alive!

Fight-or-Flight Can Save Your Life

Imagine you are walking down Fifth Avenue in Manhattan when you look up and see a grand piano falling from a fifty-fourth-story window directly toward your head. Immediately, your body reacts. Floods of stress hormones like cortisol and adrenaline are released in your brain and you are in the high-alert mode of fight-or-flight. You scramble forward a few steps and turn to watch the piano crash to the ground. You catch your breath, take a photo with your phone, and post the entire ordeal on social media. #DeathByPiano #NotTodaySteinway #ManhattanBlues.

As you walk away, you feel your body, tense as it was from being on high alert, relax again. You take another deep breath and carry on with your day. Your body's internal alarm system—anxiety—kept you safe.

The problem for many of us is that our alarm keeps sounding, even when there is no immediate threat. We walk around in fight-or-flight mode when there isn't an emergency.

A friend of mine is a firefighter and works twenty-four-hour shifts. I asked him how it's possible to routinely work twenty-four hours straight. He explained that there are lots of duties around the station, but once those are finished, if there is no emergency to attend to, they get to relax. There are beds to sleep in, video games to play, they've got a Ping-Pong table, books, and movies to keep them entertained. But the moment that alarm sounds, it's all-hands-on-deck. Everyone springs into action. I think that's a good picture of our own nervous system fluctuating between fight-or-flight and relaxation mode.

Can you picture being a firefighter when the alarm sounds at the station? Your heart rate picks up and you get ready for the emergency.

You put on your fire-resistant coat and pants. This will protect you from the heat and flames in case you get close to a fire.

You put on your boots to protect your feet and help you walk on dangerous surfaces.

You put on your gloves to protect your hands from hot surfaces and sharp objects.

You put on your helmet to protect your head from falling objects and heat.

You secure an oxygen mask to your face and strap a heavy tank of compressed air on your back so you can breathe clean air even amid a lot of smoke.

By the time you've put on all your gear, you might be carrying around an extra seventy-five pounds of equipment. Just walking around with all that gear is hard work. But it's crucial to your survival.

When you show up at that fire, you are ready to go to work putting out those flames and keeping people and pets alive. You are a literal hero. And your protective equipment keeps you safe.

That paints a pretty good picture of what happens in our nervous system when we feel anxious or stressed. Our body goes into defense mode, and we're ready to fight for our lives. Just like the firefighter's protective equipment, our body's fight-or-flight response is designed to keep us alive during threats.

Lots of high achievers struggle with anxiety. We are driven. We are ambitious. We've got a great work ethic. Those are good qualities. But there's a flip side.

After firefighters attend to an emergency, they return to the station, take off all their equipment, and go back to their day. But what if a firefighter couldn't turn off that alarm? What if they wore their protective equipment everywhere they went? What if they wore it on their first date? What if they wore it to dinner at their in-laws? What if they wore it to the movie theater or to a pickup game of basketball or to a parent-teacher meeting? Can you imagine how much that equipment would get in the way? Can you imagine how hot and bothered a person would feel all day long? Exactly this is happening to so many people today. Our bodies live in a constant state of alarm and threat. And it's time we give our bodies a break!

The good news is that you can condition your body's nervous system. When you realize your body is in a state of high alert, you can activate your relaxation mode (PNS) to calm yourself back down.

This Too Shall Pass

When the waves of anxiety are trying to drown me in their frigid waters, the first thing I do is remind myself that "this too shall pass." It helps me to remember that, even though it feels like the end of the world, no feeling lasts forever.

I also remind myself that this anxious feeling of dread and impending doom is not a premonition. This feeling doesn't mean something terrible is going to happen. This is just a feeling. And feelings can't hurt me. This puts me in the right mindset to deal with the anxiety.

Anxiety is like a huge lion in a cage roaring at you with all its might. A lion's roar is so loud that it literally makes the ground shake. It's terrifying! And that's what anxiety can feel like. Anxiety can make the ground beneath your feet feel unstable. But in keeping with this lion-in-the-cage analogy... a lion in a cage can't hurt you. All it can do is scare you. When I keep that in mind, the lyrics to the soundtrack of my day may change from this:

You aren't safe.
You'll never be safe.
Something bad is coming.

To something more like this:

You are safe.
This will not last.
You're not alone.
This too shall pass.

Reassuring Self-Talk

When it comes to self-compassion, I've learned that it's important to treat ourselves like a child for whom we are responsible. Imagine you're babysitting a six-year-old and they hear a loud noise that frightens them. What would you say to that child? I hope you would comfort them with a soothing tone. "Don't worry, it's OK. You're safe." Depending on your relationship with the child, you might even give them a hug.

The same holds true for our own anxieties. When that panic alarm goes off in our body and there's no actual danger to respond to, we need to reassure ourselves the same way we would a scared child. Place your hand on your heart and speak to yourself in the third person. My own reassuring self-talk goes like this: "Don't worry, Anthony. Everything is going to be fine. You are safe. I'm going to take care of you. What is it you need right now?"

That might sound silly, but reassuring self-talk is one of the best tools for dealing with anxiety. Give it a try! It may help immensely. And if you want to double down on the effectiveness of reassuring self-talk, add some meridian tapping in there as well.

Meridian Tapping

Meridian tapping is a technique based on the idea that we have energy pathways, called meridians, running through the body. By tapping with your fingertips on specific points along these meridians, you can stimulate energy flow and reduce physical and emotional stress. It's a simple and easy technique that you can do anywhere, and many people find it a helpful, natural way to reduce stress and promote relaxation!

In meridian tapping, you target several specific points along the body's energy pathways to release blocked energy and reduce stress.

Where to tap:

- **The eyebrow point:** located at the beginning of the eyebrow, just above the nose
- **The side of the eye:** located at the outer corner of the eye
- **Under the nose:** located between the nose and the upper lip
- **The collarbone point:** located at the center of the collarbone, near the sternum
- **The wrist point:** located on the inside of the wrist, about three finger-widths from the center of the wrist crease

Try gently tapping each area for ten to twenty seconds while practicing reassuring self-talk. See how you feel after a few minutes of meridian tapping and reassuring self-talk. It may look strange, but it always makes me feel better.

Breathing Exercises Focused on the Exhale

We've talked about how when you inhale, your heart rate quickens. When you exhale, your heart rate slows down. So, you can activate your PNS with a breathing exercise that focuses on longer exhales. Try breathing in for four seconds and breathing out for six seconds. Or try the four-seven-eight breathing exercise we explored in chapter 4 (see page 58). If you are in an environment where you can be vocal, try sighing audibly for six seconds. One study found that breathing exercises that use audible sighing were more effective than mindfulness meditation in reducing stress. Did you catch that? Sighing audibly was more effective than mindfulness meditation!

After missing a connecting flight, I was in a long customer service line at a busy airport. I always feel bad for the folks who work in customer service. It isn't their fault that we missed our flight. But there were some stressed-out people in that line. And I noticed something. Many of them were audibly sighing. And sure, they sounded whiny, but I was impressed at their instinct to audibly sigh as a way to self-regulate!

Massage Therapy

If you have health benefits at work, and one of those benefits is massage therapy, do not let that go to waste! I used to work for a large corporation that gave me benefits. And every year in December I'd realize that I hadn't used any of the money that was allocated for massage. I'd book a massage on December 17, and five minutes into the massage I'd find myself feeling so relaxed that I'd think: Why on earth haven't I been doing this more often? A good massage is one of the most deeply relaxing and restorative treatments on earth!

One of the main physiological benefits of massage therapy is that it reduces levels of the stress hormone cortisol. Massage also increases levels of serotonin and dopamine—neurotransmitters that regulate mood and promote feelings of well-being.

And that's not all! Massage stimulates blood flow and oxygenation, reduces muscle tension, and helps to release tight knots and trigger points. What else do you need? You can even give yourself a massage. Or ask a friend or partner to give you a massage. Rather than thinking of this as an indulgence, think of it as routine maintenance like you would a tune-up of a car.

Acupuncture

Acupuncture is a component of traditional Chinese medicine that involves the insertion of fine needles into specific points on the body. Because of the way it stimulates circulation, it can be used to treat injuries. But acupuncture works wonders for anxiety too. Acupuncture can activate areas of the brain that are involved in regulating emotions, including the amygdala and the hypothalamus. It can also stimulate the vagus nerve, which is responsible for activating the PNS and helping the body to relax. And learning to relax is a big deal—especially for high performers.

What Works for One Won't Work for All

Before we close this chapter, I want to remind you that there is no one-size-fits-all tool for dealing with anxiety. For folks with a history of trauma, stillness exercises like meditation and breathwork may be overwhelming. If that's you, please know this is perfectly normal. Go at your own pace and find the tools that work for you. Sometimes the best thing you can do is reach out to a therapist or counselor who can help you with your specific situation. Some people may find a therapist trained in somatics or embodiment especially helpful. Please know that you're worth it—you deserve the right care and treatment for your well-being.

Sometimes my own anxiety feels like something I should keep secret. I used to feel as though admitting I deal with anxiety made me weak. But now I see that seeking treatment is an expression of courage. It requires self-compassion. I hope you'll try some of these tools for dealing with anxiety. But if these don't work for you, try not to be discouraged.

One of the most repeated sayings in psychology circles is this: "Never worry alone." When you are overwhelmed with anxiety, don't suffer in silence. Take care of yourself the way you would take care of a child you are responsible for. Give yourself heaps and heaps of self-compassion. Reassure your inner child. And reach out for help when you need it.

GET ALL FIRED UP!

Optimize mental wellness: Decide on a course of action for the next time your body is carrying anxiety. Breathing exercises are a great choice because they can be performed anywhere. Practice four-seven-eight breathing now so you can access it when you really need it.

Ignite joy: One way to soothe anxiety (and there are many ways) is to use reassuring self-talk. Write some lyrics to a new soundtrack that you find calming.

Fuel peak performance: Go get a massage. Seriously, do it!

7

THE BODY-BRAIN CONNECTION

I'm sorry for what I said when I was hungry.

GABRIEL IGLESIAS

M Y INTEREST in mental performance began with a passion to function at my best, for the longest amount of time, with the least amount of wear and tear. All my focus was on mental performance. I noticed the impact of meditation on my ability to focus for longer amounts of time. I observed the way breathing exercises cleared my head at the end of a difficult task. I saw my confidence improve as I learned self-compassion skills during therapy sessions. But something else kept popping up that surprised me.

Throughout my research on high performance, I kept hearing about the role the physical body plays in mental health. In fact, you can't really separate your mental health from your physical body. As I thought about what this looked like in my own life, I realized how often my physical health was influencing my mood, energy levels, and overall wellness.

How many times have I felt irritable and cranky when all I needed was a snack?

How many times have I felt tired and sluggish when all I needed was to go for a walk?

How many times have I felt overwhelmed and exhausted when all I needed was a nap?

And how many times have I had a headache when all I needed was a glass of water?

There have been times when I felt like quitting my job, selling my possessions, and moving to a wood cabin in the Costa Rican rainforest when all I really needed was a good night's sleep. So now, anytime I'm feeling off-center, I check my compass. Nutrition, exercise, sleep, and water are crucial for well-being.

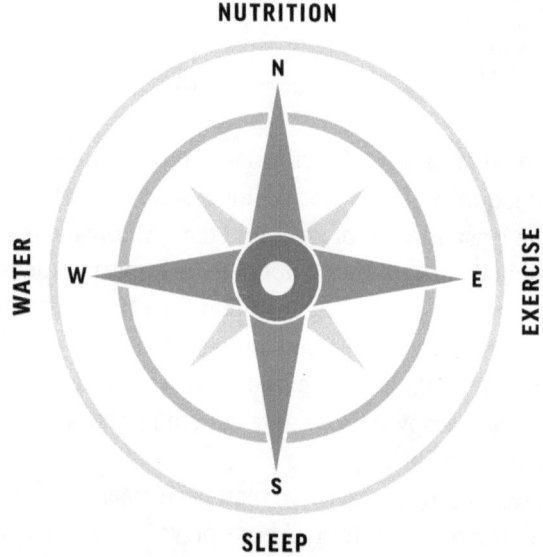

Take a picture of this image. Anytime you feel overwhelmed, ask yourself the body-brain compass questions:

- How's my nutrition?
- Am I moving my body?
- Am I sleeping well?
- Am I drinking enough water?

Before you quit your job and move to the rainforest, try focusing on these key points of well-being. That can be a game-changer! Let's break down each one of these compass points, as well as a few other key elements that live at the intersection of physical wellness and mental health.

Nutrition

Most of us know that eating a healthy diet is an important part of overall physical health. But we often don't realize what a huge influence nutrition has on mental health! Your brain needs a variety of nutrients to function properly, and when you don't get enough of those nutrients, your mood, energy levels, and cognitive function can suffer.

So, what are the key nutrients that can support your mental health? Here are a few:

- **Omega-3 fatty acids:** These healthy fats are found in fatty fish, nuts, and seeds, and have been linked to improved cognitive function and a reduced risk of depression.

- **B vitamins:** B vitamins are important for energy production and can help reduce symptoms of depression and anxiety. You can find them in whole grains, leafy greens, and lean proteins.

- **Antioxidants:** These powerful compounds protect your brain cells from damage and inflammation. You can find them in colorful fruits and vegetables, as well as in green tea and dark chocolate.

Now, on the flip side, a poor diet can negatively affect your mental health. A diet that is lacking in essential nutrients, such as vitamins and minerals, can lead to fatigue, low energy levels, and a lack of motivation. You don't need that in your life right now! And hey, you don't have to make drastic changes to your diet to reap the benefits of good nutrition. Small steps can make a big difference. Here are a few ideas to get you started:

- Swap out sugary drinks for water or herbal tea. Staying hydrated can help you feel more alert and focused.

- Include a serving of fruits or vegetables with every meal. This can help you get more of the vitamins and minerals your brain needs to function at its best.
- Get those healthy fats! Try including avocado, coconut, or olive oil in your daily routine. Your brain will thank you!
- Experiment with new healthy recipes. Eating well doesn't have to be boring or bland. Try out some new dishes and see what you enjoy!

Remember, the goal is progress, not perfection. Don't beat yourself up if you slip up and eat a less-than-healthy meal or snack. The key is to focus on making small, sustainable changes that you can stick with over time. By fueling your body with the right nutrients, you can boost your mood, increase your energy levels, and support your cognitive function. So, take a step toward better nutrition, and see how it can improve your overall well-being!

Exercise

Everyone knows that exercise, much like proper nutrition, is good for your physical health. It can help you maintain a healthy weight, lower your blood pressure, and reduce your risk of chronic diseases. But some days, that still isn't enough to get us moving! So, let's talk about the incredible benefits that physical exercise can have on your mental health.

First and foremost, exercise is a powerful mood-booster. When you engage in physical activity, your brain releases endorphins, those feel-good chemicals that make you feel happier, more positive, and more relaxed. In fact, studies have shown that regular exercise can be just as effective as medication or therapy for treating symptoms of mild to moderate depression.

Regular exercise can also improve your energy levels and overall sense of well-being. When you're physically active, your body gets better at using oxygen and nutrients, so you feel more alert and focused. Plus, exercise improves sleep, which also contributes to higher energy levels and a more positive outlook on life.

Exercise has social benefits as well. When my family and I moved to a new city recently, we found that one of the best ways to meet people is playing sports! Earlier this year, someone invited me to an afternoon playing a sport I had never tried before—pickleball. My first instinct was to say no. After all, I've never played before, what if I was terrible at it? What if I just embarrassed myself? But then I remembered—it's not about the sport. It's about connecting with people. It's about social bonding. So, I went and played pickleball for the first time. And can I tell you... I loved it! I think it's my new favorite sport! It's kind of like tennis, only the court is smaller so it's not quite as physically demanding. If anyone invites you to play the fastest-growing sport in North America, say yes!

Another great way to connect with new friends is to go on a hike. Physical activity can be fun! You don't have to go to the gym or lift weights if that's not your thing. Some of us get intimidated if we don't have an athletic body or aren't confident enough to take an intense class. Don't let "big fitness" rob you of the joy of movement. Find an activity that you look forward to and that makes you feel good.

And remember, exercise doesn't have to be all-or-nothing. Even small amounts of physical activity can have a big effect on your mental health. Taking a short walk during your lunch break, doing some gentle yoga before bed, or dancing around your living room to your favorite song are great ways to get moving and boost your mood.

So even if you haven't been active as of late, give exercise a try. You might be surprised at how much happier, more energized, and more connected to the world you feel. Start small, be consistent, and have fun with it. Your mental health will thank you!

Sleep

You are exercising regularly. You are eating a healthy diet. You see a therapist twice a week. You spend time gardening. You earn enough money to pay all your bills and go on two vacations a year. You have a wonderful family. But if you are only getting two or three hours of sleep every night, how do you feel? Miserable. There is no way around it—sleep influences your overall well-being like nothing else. Sleep may be the most important and the most neglected component of good mental health. Let's break down why sleep is such a game-changer.

Getting enough high-quality sleep is essential for your brain and body to function at their best. When you're well-rested, you're more alert, focused, and able to manage stress and difficult emotions. On the other hand, a lack of sleep can have serious consequences for your mental health and overall well-being.

So, what are some of the benefits of getting enough sleep? Here are a few:

- Improved mood: Studies have shown that getting enough sleep can reduce symptoms of depression and anxiety, and help you feel more positive and optimistic.

- Better concentration: When you're well-rested, you're better able to focus on tasks and maintain your attention, which can improve your productivity and performance.

- Increased creativity: Sleep is essential for allowing your brain to consolidate memories and make new connections, which can boost your creativity and problem-solving abilities.

Anytime you're feeling off-center, check your compass: nutrition, exercise, sleep, and water are crucial for well-being.

- Enhanced physical health: Getting enough sleep is linked to a lower risk of chronic diseases like heart disease, diabetes, and obesity.

On the other hand, a lack of sleep can have serious negative consequences for your mental health. Let's start with mood. When you don't get enough sleep, you are more likely to feel irritable, moody, and anxious. Studies have shown that sleep deprivation can make us more reactive to negative emotions and less able to cope with stress. One study found that people who slept less than six hours per night were more likely to report symptoms of depression and anxiety than those who slept more.

My motivation levels go way down when I'm not getting enough sleep. I'm irritable with my kids, I'm ineffective at work, and I'm no fun to be around. My overall quality of life suffers. So, how can you improve your sleep habits and reap the benefits of better rest? Here are a few tips:

- **Stick to a regular sleep schedule:** Try to go to bed and wake up at roughly the same times every day, even on weekends. This can help regulate your body's natural sleep-wake cycle. And if you are staying awake later, make sure it's because you are doing truly life-affirming activities. For example, if I'm having an awesome night out with friends, staying up late might be worth it. But sometimes I'm up late just mindlessly scrolling on my phone. And I never feel good about the lack of sleep the next day. Be honest with yourself about why you are staying up late. And prioritize going to bed.

- **Create a relaxing bedtime routine:** Take a warm bath, read a book, light some candles, or do some gentle stretching before bed to calm your mind and signal to your body that it's time to sleep.

- **Make your bedroom a sleep-friendly environment:** Keep your bedroom cool, dark, and quiet, and invest in a comfortable mattress and pillows.

- **Avoid screens before bed:** The blue light emitted by electronic devices can disrupt your sleep, so try to avoid using them for at least an hour before bedtime.

Look, getting enough sleep is one of the most important things you can do for your mental health. By prioritizing rest and relaxation, you can reap the benefits of a better mood, improved concentration, and overall well-being. Plus, you'll be more fun to be around! So, for the sake of your own mental health, and for the sake of your family and friends, make sleep a priority!

Water

You know your body is 60 percent water, right? You know up to 50 percent of all headaches are caused by dehydration, right? You know you need to be drinking more water—but let me get you excited about drinking more water! Look at these benefits:

- Increased energy: When you're properly hydrated, your body can function more efficiently, which can help you feel more alert and energized throughout the day.

- Improved mood: Dehydration can lead to feelings of fatigue and irritability, while proper hydration can help you feel more positive and upbeat.

- Enhanced cognitive function: Drinking enough water can improve your concentration, memory, and ability to stay focused on tasks.

- Boosted physical performance: Proper hydration can help your muscles work more efficiently, which can improve your endurance and athletic performance.

Think of a plant that is getting enough water. It's green and flourishing—it's living its best life! Now picture a shriveled-up plant that hasn't been watered in months. Those are pictures of what's happening to you when you drink water and when you are dehydrated. I don't want you looking like a shrub on the side of the road in the desert in the middle of July. I want you to look like a red fern in the rainforest! I want you flourishing!

When you're dehydrated, you feel sluggish and unmotivated and have difficulty focusing on tasks. Sometimes you won't even realize why you're feeling so lethargic. If you want to avoid the blahs, stay hydrated!

By drinking enough water, you will boost your energy, improve your mood, and enhance your cognitive function. Why not have a glass of water right now?!

Let the Sunlight In

Music sounds better when the sun is shining. The birds sing louder when the sun is shining. If the barista gets my order wrong, it isn't so bad when the sun is shining. Why does it feel like everything's a little better when the sun is shining? It turns out, there's science behind that.

Sunlight helps your body make vitamin D, which is important for keeping your brain and nerves healthy. Plus, it helps regulate your circadian rhythm (your body's natural sleep schedule), which gives you your sleep and wake cues. And sunlight boosts the production of serotonin (recall, that's a "happy hormone"). But wait! There's more! (Cue the infomercial music, please.)

Studies have suggested that adequate vitamin D levels may also protect against cognitive decline and may be beneficial in preventing neurological conditions such as multiple sclerosis, Alzheimer's disease, and Parkinson's disease. We are only beginning to understand the profound impact sunlight has on our brains.

Getting an adequate amount of sunlight and vitamin D is crucial to overall mental health. Within the first hour of waking up, try to get some natural sunlight. And of course, don't overdo it! Overexposure to the sun leads to sunburn, and staring directly into the noonday sun is bad for your eyes. Please use common sense when hanging with our celestial neighbor.

If you live in an area where it's hard to get natural sunlight, or if you work in an office where sunlight is scarce, I highly recommend getting a light therapy lamp. Light therapy lamps (sometimes called vitamin D lamps) give off UV light which helps your skin make vitamin D. Many people who suffer from seasonal affective disorder (SAD) have reported huge improvements in their mood, energy levels, and sleep and wake cycles when they regularly use a light therapy lamp. If you find yourself feeling low in the winter months, give it a try!

More Magnesium, Please

A few years back, I had a rough patch in my parenting journey. I was feeling grumpy, irritable, and constantly on edge with my kids. I had zero patience, and it felt like I was always one step away from losing my cool. Why was I always down to my last nerve? Like, seriously, what happened to all my other nerves?

One day I was sharing all this with my brother, and he suggested that I might have a magnesium deficiency. He said that one of the telltale signs is irritability. He told me to look into taking an over-the-counter magnesium supplement to see if it might help. I was a bit skeptical at first, but I figured I'd give it a shot. So, I started taking 300 milligrams of magnesium glycinate every day. And a funny thing happened... I finally felt like there was a buffer between me and my last nerve. Parenting still has its fair share of frustrations, but I was noticeably less irritable. Magnesium has made such a big difference in my household that Susie and I jokingly refer to it as the "parenting supplement." I still take it every day!

Gut Health

Did you know that your gut health and microbiome have a huge impact on your overall mental health and well-being? The trillions of microorganisms that live in your gut play a crucial role in everything from mood and stress to anxiety and depression. And if that's not enough to get you excited about gut health, consider this: research has shown that the microbiome may even impact things like weight loss, skin health, and longevity. We are just scratching the surface when it comes to understanding the ecosystem within our gut!

You don't need to understand all the science to reap the benefits of a healthy microbiome. First and foremost, focus on eating a healthy, balanced diet that is rich in fiber, whole foods, and probiotics. This means lots of fruits, veggies, and fermented foods like yogurt, kefir, and sauerkraut. These foods provide the nutrients and beneficial bacteria that your gut needs to thrive. I also take a probiotic supplement of fifty billion CFUs (colony-forming units) to boost my microbiome each day. Look into the benefits for yourself.

GET ALL FIRED UP!

Optimize mental wellness: Physical health is closely tied to mental well-being. Check your body-brain compass and notice where there may be room to improve your habits.

Ignite joy: The next time the sun is shining, get out in it! Go for a walk, stand soaking up a few rays, feel its warm heat for a few minutes.

Fuel peak performance: Take a nap! Just nap!

8

THE CONFIDENCE FACTOR

Confidence is not "will they like me?"
Confidence is "I'll be fine if they don't."

CHRISTINA GRIMMIE

PEOPLE ASK me if I still get nervous before a big keynote speech. My reply is always the same: I've spoken at thousands of events, and I *still get nervous* before each one. But that nervous energy can become fuel—it can turn into adrenaline. So being nervous isn't always a bad thing.

But there are times when being nervous spills over into self-doubt and anxiety. That's not helpful at all. There are other times when imposter syndrome has really knocked me off my game. It seems to happen to me every time I move up a level. Let me explain...

When I was speaking in schools, I gave hundreds of talks to students on the subject of bullying. I spent years gleaning best practices from teachers, administrators, parents, child psychologists... I knew that what I was sharing had value and could make a difference. And I was getting great feedback from schools. One day a school invited me to share my material with a new audience: teachers. I was excited about the opportunity, and we booked a date.

That's when the imposter syndrome started whispering to me... Teachers?! Who am I to speak to teachers? I can't teach a group of teachers. They're *grown-ups*! Sure, kids will listen to me... but adults won't. And I'm not even a teacher! What makes me think I can speak to them?! Imposter syndrome started as a whisper but quickly became a shout. I was terrified. But it was too late—I'd already booked the date. I couldn't back out now.

So, I did what I always do. I researched. I prepared. I rehearsed. And when I spoke for that group of teachers... it was great! They loved it. They didn't judge me or look down on me. They wanted to hear from me. I conquered my imposter syndrome. Or so I thought. But then...

I got invited to speak for a group of vice principals. And again, imposter syndrome started whispering... I can't speak to school administrators! They wear business clothes! They probably all have advanced doctorate degrees. I don't have an advanced doctorate degree! Who am I to teach them anything?! Why would they want to hear from me?!?!

When I took the stage, I was shaking with fear and anxiety. I gave my talk, and it was decent—but it could have been so much better if I were confident in my material instead of fearful of their judgment. I ended up working with some of those same vice principals for years, and I discovered they are normal people just like anyone else. And they themselves go through imposter syndrome and self-doubt too. I wish I knew then what I know now: every time you move up a level, there will be doubt, there will be fear, but you've got what it takes!

Confidence Is a Game-Changer

Confidence can be the difference between success or failure in any given endeavor. You can have all the skills in the world, but if you don't have confidence—a deep-seated trust in your own abilities—you don't have what it takes to reach your goals. Let me explain what I mean...

Let's say you're interviewing for a job or going for a promotion that you are fully qualified for. If you are confident in your abilities, you are going to rock that interview! You'll answer questions clearly, you'll share ideas freely, and you'll pick up on vibes in the room. Why? Because you are fully present. You are so confident in your abilities, you don't have to worry about how you're coming across to your interviewers. You know you have what it takes, and you belong in that role! You are going to make a great impression in the room.

But what happens in that same interview if you aren't sure of yourself? You second-guess your answers. You waver. You doubt yourself. You give off an unsteady vibe. You are so worried about how you must be coming across to the interviewer that you don't pick up on vibes in the room. You aren't sure if you have what it takes... and now they feel the same way.

Ironically, you might be the right person for the job. You might have all the necessary skills. But a lack of confidence sends out the wrong signals, and you miss out on that job or promotion. Sometimes it's not your skill set that needs to change, it's your confidence in your skill set that needs to change.

How Do You Build Confidence?

The number one key to building confidence is preparation. When you are prepared, you feel more confident because you know that you've done everything you can to succeed. The more you prepare, the more confident you will feel. I'll tell you what this looks like in my work as a keynote speaker.

Confidence is a by-product of predictability. The more predictable a speaking event, the more confident I feel. My incredible booking team handles all my speaking gigs. And before my feet hit that stage, my team has set me up for success by making things as predictable as possible. Each client has sent over a questionnaire that includes the exact date, time, and location of the event, the title of the talk I am giving, the name and address of my hotel, the size of the audience,

Be confident but stay hungry. Keep working hard and don't take success for granted.

the dress code for the event, the available A/V equipment, and a tech rehearsal time.

I have a pre-event call with every client too. I meet the team behind the event and learn more about their organization. I also ask two key questions before any event: What do you want participants to be thinking about as they leave my presentation? How do you want them to feel?

If I have a good idea of what the event planner wants participants to think and feel as they leave, I have set myself up for success. I also use the power of visualization.

Visualization

You may have heard of Fu Mingxia, the legendary Chinese diver and Olympic athlete. She was such an incredible diver that she qualified for her first Olympic Games at just thirteen years old. Everything was looking good until she broke her foot during a training session leading up to the Olympic Games. She was devastated. The doctors told her she had to wear a cast and couldn't train in the water for weeks. When you are competing at that level, so close to the big event, missing a single day of practice can be detrimental, let alone several weeks.

Instead of telling her to pull out of the competition, her coaches encouraged Fu Mingxia to try visualization. She showed up at the pool every day and pictured herself doing her dives with perfect form and technique. She stood at the pool's edge, closed her eyes, and mentally rehearsed every twist, every turn, every detail of the dive. She saw herself performing that dive perfectly thousands of times.

Finally, her cast was removed. She only had a short amount of time before her Olympic debut. Most people counted her out. She was just thirteen years old and had missed so many crucial weeks of training. But Fu Mingxia didn't listen to the doubters. She just kept picturing herself performing a perfect dive. All that visualization paid off—she went on to win the gold medal in the women's platform event at the 1992 Olympic Games.

Fu Mingxia mentally rehearsed a perfect dive over and over again. My question for you is, What are you mentally rehearsing? What's the picture you have in your own mind? When you vividly imagine yourself performing a task well, you are going to improve your focus, increase your confidence, and train your brain to perform at its best.

I want you to channel your inner Fu Mingxia. She physically went to the pool and stood by the water to visualize herself. She smelled the chlorine, she saw the height of the diving board. That's how specific you should be when you are practicing visualization.

Let's say you are gearing up for an important pitch meeting. Picture the big day. Where will the meeting take place? On a video call at home? In someone else's office? What time of day is it happening? What will you eat that day? Will you drink coffee/tea? When? What about your outfit—what will you be wearing?

In theater, actors rehearse in their costume shoes because it adds another layer of authenticity. That's the level of detail I recommend when you visualize. Put on the outfit and the shoes you're going to be wearing and go through your pitch again and again—it makes a difference. In French, the word for "rehearsal" is "répétition." Nothing takes the place of practice. You want to run through your routine as many times as possible so it feels almost predictable. That level of preparation will boost your confidence for sure.

Preparation That Will Boost Your Confidence

Pitch meetings are a big part of my work as a filmmaker. Movies cost millions of dollars to finance, and they can take years to put together. And it all starts with a pitch meeting where you share your idea with an executive. A meeting with a Hollywood executive might only last fifteen minutes. If it goes well, they have the power to get you one step closer to that green light. So, every pitch is a huge opportunity.

The film I am developing now is called *Earthquake Prom*. It's about an earthquake that strikes right in the middle of a high school prom. Four students from very different social circles find themselves trapped in a room. As they struggle to escape, they realize they have more in common than their social status would suggest. I wrote the screenplay, and I'm hoping to direct the movie as well. I have a small team of producers, and together we're setting up meetings to pitch the film. We have a pitch deck, we shot a "proof of concept" scene to give investors a feel for the movie, and I have a seven-minute pitch about the film. That part makes me nervous. In seven minutes, can I capture the magic of this film? I want to be confident when I step into those meetings! So, here's what I've been doing to prepare...

I wrote the entire pitch, shared it with the team, got feedback, and rewrote it again. Once I had the written pitch locked down, I memorized it. I ran through the pitch while driving, while in the shower, while washing dishes. That's where I'm at now, and I feel like I'm ready. But Shonda Rhimes, the prolific film and TV mogul, says that you need to be able to deliver your entire pitch at double speed, with loud music playing, before you're truly ready. *That* is the level of preparation that I'm talking about! And that's the level of preparation that will boost your confidence.

A deep level of preparation allows you to roll with the flow no matter how a meeting is going. An executive I'm pitching to might have a crying infant in their lap. The executive may leave for a few minutes right in the middle of the pitch. Or they might want more information about a side character. Expect the unexpected! And if I've rehearsed under various conditions, I'll be prepared to roll with the punches.

There's another thing I'm going to do for these meetings, and I recommend it for your big events as well.

Be Early

Maybe you're going to pitch a project to your boss, give a company-wide presentation, or have a coffee meeting with the CEO... always be early! Never make the mistake of getting there on time. Give yourself the opportunity to find parking and use the bathroom and review your notes and allow your heart rate to settle down before the big event. If you're running late, or making it just barely on time, you're going to arrive feeling flustered and disoriented. That can distract you from giving your best performance or making a great first impression.

Rituals for Peak Performance

When preparing for a big moment, a set of rituals can help you get in the right mindset and feel more confident. Whether you're delivering a speech, sharing a new strategy in a business meeting, pitching a movie idea, or preparing to sing the national anthem at a huge stadium, developing a routine can mentally prepare you and clear your mind.

Your ritual might involve meditation, mantras, a power pose (arms extended overhead works for me!), or a vocal warm-up.

Your ritual might also involve listening to a specific playlist. My wife, Susie, likes to blast the Eminem song "Lose Yourself" when she's heading into a big audition. The key is to create a unique routine that focuses and centers you. By repeating the same actions every time you prepare for a big moment, you'll create a sense of familiarity and control that can ease your nerves and boost your confidence.

The Power of Mantras

I shared about mantras in an earlier chapter, but they are worth revisiting. A mantra is a word or phrase that you repeat again and again to focus the mind. Lots of successful people use mantras to refine their focus and boost their confidence before a high-pressure situation. Legendary conductor Leonard Bernstein used the mantra "I deserve to be here" backstage before a concert. Another conductor, Gustavo Dudamel, takes a deep breath and says to himself, "This is going to be great."

I use mantras every time my imposter syndrome starts whispering to me. If I feel nervous about speaking to a particular group—it could be a gathering of business leaders or a group of college professors—I remind myself that I was invited to be there. And one of the mantras that has been most helpful is this:

"If they wanted someone else, they could have chosen someone else, but they chose me, so I will be myself."

When I repeat that to myself, the imposter syndrome gets weaker, my confidence grows stronger, and I can focus on the task at hand: serving this group!

That brings me to an important point. When I shift my focus from the self-centered question "What will they think of me?" to "How can I help these people?" my thoughts instantly go from anxious worrying to interest in the present moment. The next time you speak in public, focus on the importance of the material you are sharing. You aren't there for admiration; you are here to serve people. Confidence isn't a tool to gain admiration; it is a fuel to serve people.

Avoid Overconfidence

Finally, in a chapter about confidence, I'd like to mention that you can definitely be overly confident. I've seen people so sure of their skills that they feel like they don't need to practice, so full of swagger that they think they don't need to prepare. That's a huge mistake. Be confident but stay hungry. Keep working hard and don't take success for granted.

GET ALL FIRED UP!

Optimize mental wellness: Being nervous isn't necessarily a bad thing. Ground your nervousness by channeling the energy into top-notch preparation, and then harness the adrenaline to deliver a great performance.

Ignite joy: Develop a simple confidence-boosting ritual to do before any event where you need to be at your best.

Fuel peak performance: What's your confidence mantra? Write it down and stick it somewhere you'll see it often.

9
RELATION-
SHIPS

A friend is someone who knows the song in your heart and can sing it back to you when you have forgotten the words.

C.S. LEWIS

WE ALL know relationships are important, and we learned that especially during the pandemic when we couldn't see our loved ones as often. Positive social connections are one of the best ways to boost your overall mental wellness. I need people. You need people. We are hardwired for connection. Parts of the brain are dormant until we interact with others. The so-called love hormone, oxytocin, is released when you bond with others. Oxytocin calms your nervous system, boosts your positivity, and lowers your blood pressure.

The novelist Ann Hood said, "I have learned that there is more power in a good strong hug than in a thousand meaningful words." Keep in mind, this is coming from someone who makes her living with words. But a good strong hug works wonders. When you hug someone you feel safe with, oxytocin floods your body. And oxytocin reduces the production of cortisol (the stress hormone) and triggers the release of other feel-good hormones like serotonin. A twenty-second hug will boost your overall wellness like nothing else on earth.

Oxytocin is also released when we spend quality time with a pet. I learned this early in life with the greatest dog ever, a golden retriever named Bonnie. We got Bonnie when I was just four years old. My parents had recently divorced, and my brother, sister, and I moved with my mom to a new town. It was a new beginning filled with uncertainty, but Bonnie made all the difference in the world. Dogs are a source of unconditional love. They can run with you in the park and cuddle with you on the couch. They can even feel your emotions and comfort you when you are down. In fact, service dogs have been proven to be effective in reducing symptoms of post-traumatic stress disorder among military veterans. A study at Purdue University found that veterans partnered with service dogs had lower levels of depression, less anxiety, and more willingness to participate in social events.

In 2019, a study of over ten thousand adults in the US found that three out of five Americans are lonely. And loneliness rates increased 13 percent from 2018 to 2019. This was before the pandemic and all the isolation that came along with it! Despite all our cell phones, social media, dating apps, and tools for connection, we are lonelier now than ever. We need to talk about relationships!

The truth is, no matter how much of a high performer you want to be in your career, you still need people to connect with outside your work. We must take a more holistic view of our lives. We can get so ambitious in our careers that we sacrifice meaningful relationships in our personal lives. I encourage you to tap into friendships as a source of strength and inspiration that you can bring with you.

Meaningful Connection

Relationships are built on meaningful connections. But issues from the past can get in the way of forming these connections.

A few months back, I met a business leader in Chicago who shared his story with me. He grew up in one of the toughest parts of the city. Whether from a raging father inside his house or from the gang members outside his front door, he was constantly in danger. He made it through by being tough, building a shell around himself that nobody could break. He kept his softer side hidden. He knew that a good education could help him escape from his situation. He worked hard at school, went to college on a scholarship, and later earned an MBA. He landed a job at a Fortune 500 company and climbed the ladder, getting better jobs over time. He also got married and had two children. From the outside, his life looked perfect. But there was a problem.

He still had that tough shell around him. His wife found him emotionally distant, and he struggled to connect with his children. The walls he built as a child to protect himself were now barriers that kept his family at a distance.

His story resonated with me. Although I didn't grow up in a rough neighborhood, I did develop coping skills as a child that worked against me as an adult. My issue was not getting enough attention as a kid. I discovered that impressing people and being charming, funny, and outgoing earned me the attention I craved. However, as an adult, this type of performance in social situations can be off-putting. It can seem fake. Real friendship isn't about impressing people, it's about making a deep connection. To develop meaningful relationships, I had to drop the performance.

That business leader and I shared a connection that day. We had both developed coping skills as kids that were hindering us as adults. If you find this rings true for you as well, I encourage you to consider talking to a trained therapist about it. That's what I suggested to my friend in Chicago. If therapy is not currently feasible for you financially, you can research "Internal Family Systems" online to explore what resonates. Throughout your journey, be kind to your inner child, who developed those coping mechanisms for protection. Remember that practicing self-compassion will serve your recovery far better than feeling shame for the survival strategies of a child who was doing their best.

High Performers Tend to Hide Pain

Recently, I was shocked by the sudden death of a very successful man in my industry. I never got the chance to know him personally, but I followed his career with great admiration. He was talented, hardworking, and he lit up any room he was in with his positive energy. On social media, he posted pictures and videos of his family, and he seemed to have the work-life balance thing figured out quite well. Those who knew him were devastated by his sudden death. What shocked me most was that he died by suicide. It turns out he suffered in silence for years. He never shared any of his struggles with the people he worked with. Even his friends and family didn't know about his battle with depression. How many other high performers are suffering in silence? How many successful people feel unable to speak up about their own struggles?

I watched a documentary about another highly successful person who died by suicide, the celebrated chef Anthony Bourdain. The documentary revealed that because Bourdain was so successful in his career, he felt he had no right to complain about his personal well-being. He knew others were suffering from financial burdens or physical ailments, and he felt guilty addressing his own emotional pain since he had so much in terms of wealth and resources. So he suffered in silence. He focused on work and tried to ignore his depression. To the outside world, he was living the dream. But his inner world was tormented by hopelessness and despair. And no one knew the extent of his pain until his death in a French hotel.

High performers often suffer in silence. Celebrated for their success, they feel unable to open up about their weaknesses. I don't want that to be you. It is imperative that you have relationships in your life where you can be completely open and honest. And if you don't have those relationships, I highly recommend finding a therapist or counselor. Keep in mind, unless they believe you may harm yourself or another person, these professionals are legally bound to keep your conversations confidential. This rule allows you to share openly and honestly, knowing your personal matters won't leave the confines of your sessions. Whether you get support from a therapist, family member, or close friend, it is essential you aren't going through struggles on your own.

Three Safe Contacts

I'm going to ask you to identify three safe contacts you can reach out to in an emergency. When life spirals out of control, you need to know who you can talk to about your most intimate secrets. And these are people outside your romantic relationships. Let me explain the idea behind the three safe contacts.

Every time you board an airplane, the flight attendants go through the safety protocols: In an emergency, here's where you can find your safety vest. If the plane lands in water, here are the emergency exits where the inflatable slides will be. Most flight attendants will never need to use the inflatable slide, but every flight attendant knows where to find them if they need them.

This is exactly what we're doing with our three safe contacts. Hopefully, we'll never be in an emergency that warrants our reaching out to them. But we know exactly who they are and how to reach them if we need to.

Who can you talk to when you just lost your house in a bad gambling bet?

Who can you call when your partner just found out about the affair? Or you found out about theirs?

When you're alone in a hotel room and you're contemplating a choice that cannot be reversed, who can you call?

I want you to have three safe contacts that you can call day or night, no matter the circumstances. Determine who those people are right now. Reach out to them today. Ask them if they will be your safe contact in an emergency. Promise them that if you ever go through extreme hardship and feel like doing something catastrophic like suicide, you will reach out to one of them, day or night, no matter the time. And offer to be their safe contact if they need one.

It might seem strange to talk about horrible emergencies when you aren't dealing with one. But the best time to buy a fire extinguisher is not during a fire. The best time to prepare for the worst time is right now. You can't wait until your life is spiraling out of control to figure out who you can trust with your greatest difficulties. You need three safe contacts. And remember—none of them should be a romantic partner. Let me explain why.

A healthy romantic relationship is one of the great joys in life. But if you have a partner and that person is the only one who knows your inner struggles, you are putting way too much pressure on them. They should be just one of the people who know about your dark side. There are also times when opening up to a romantic partner may feel too vulnerable, or you may not want to burden them. Sometimes it is easier to open up to someone you don't share a bank account with. So, while I hope you can open up to your romantic partner about everything you go through, your three safe contacts are above and beyond this person. If one of your safe contacts becomes a romantic partner, you need another safe contact.

Please, never go through hardships alone. Never suffer in silence. Reach out for help. And decide right now who are your three safe contacts. If you feel you may not have three people you could ask to be your safe contacts, identify different crisis support resources. Depending on where you live, there may be a crisis phone number, text service, or app that you can access in an emergency. Just make sure you have a total of three safe contacts. I don't want you to wait until you are in a crisis to access those services. Find them now so they are there when you need them.

When it comes to your three safe contacts, that word "safe" is key. You may have some friendships or relationships that are not quite healthy. Let's explore some warning signs for unhealthy relationships.

Red Flags for Relationships

Here are some possible warning signs that you are not in a healthy relationship. By "relationship," I mean with a friend, romantic partner, colleague, or family member. If this person is a colleague, you might still have to see them every day. If they are a distant relative, you might still have to see them on holidays. A red flag doesn't mean you need to end the relationship, it just means be careful how close you let them in. Some red flags are obvious:

- Do they gossip about you?
- Do they lie to you?
- Do they get jealous when you spend time with other people?
- Do they refuse to take accountability and apologize for their actions?

But other red flags require a bit more unpacking...

Let's say something good happens in your life: you get a promotion at work, or you get engaged to the love of your life, or you are recognized for a project well done. When you share your good news with this person, how do they react? Are they genuinely happy for you? Or do they seem threatened and insecure? Do they subtly insult you? Do they diminish your accomplishment? Do they question why good things happen for you?

Let's say you are a woman who just got a promotion at work. You share the news with a friend who says, "They've been trying to promote more women at the workplace, so it makes sense that you'd get this promotion." That is a huge red flag. That person just diminished your accomplishment. You just saw the fin of the shark. It may seem small, but the fin you see above the surface belongs to a much bigger shark below the surface. If someone diminishes your accomplishments, that is a clear warning. In a healthy relationship, we celebrate each other's wins.

How Do You Feel after Spending Time Together?

How I feel after I've spent time with someone is a very helpful metric for me. I love the quote from C.S. Lewis that opens this chapter: "A friend is someone who knows the song in your heart and can sing it back to you when you have forgotten the words."

Those are the friendships I want in my life. And that's the type of friend I want to be. When I walk away from time spent with a friend, I want to be reminded of who I am and who I want to be. So, pay attention to how you feel after you've spent time with someone.

When you walk away from a visit:

A. Are you hoping you won't see them again for a very long time?

or

B. Are you looking forward to the next time you'll see them?

When you hang up the phone:

A. Do you feel refreshed?

or

B. Do you feel drained?

Employees who have close friendships at work are **seven times more likely to be engaged in their jobs.**

Of course, we all go through difficult seasons, and sometimes you may walk away from a conversation from even the best of friends feeling heavy. By no means should you be a "fair-weather friend" who only wants to be there for the good times. Being a true friend means walking with people through their worst days and celebrating with them on their best days. I have spent time with people going through hardships and I always feel a deep sense of appreciation that they would share their most difficult struggles with me. And even in the pain, I can feel the joy of our connection. Holding someone in their brokenness is one of the most powerful moments of friendship.

That being said, some people are in a never-ending cycle of crisis. If your relationship revolves around you rescuing them from their latest crisis, you might want to rethink how much time and energy you are investing in that relationship.

Do They Respect Your Boundaries?

Every relationship needs boundaries. And for a relationship to be healthy, both parties must respect those boundaries. Let me give you an example...

Let's say a friend invites you over for a late dinner. The problem is that you are exhausted, and you really need to stay home to rest and recharge. So you tell them it won't work and that you need an early night. How does your friend respond?

Do they become angry?
Do they bring it up later to make you feel guilty?
Do they use passive-aggressive behavior to try to shame you?
Do they make it weird?

You don't really know a person until you see how they react when you say no to them. And a healthy relationship is one in which both parties respect each other's nos.

If someone doesn't want to drink, no one should pressure them to drink. If someone doesn't want to date a certain person, no one should pressure them to date that person. This should be obvious but check your circle. Is everyone on the same page with respecting boundaries?

Safe Senders List

When I get email spammed by a company or when someone is phishing for my bank password or trying to sell me on a training program I'm not interested in, I flag the email and send it to the trash. I flag it so that the next time that sender tries to spam me, it goes directly to my spam folder. That contact is not on my "safe senders" list.

But let's say I go to a new store, and I love their products and I sign up for their newsletter because I genuinely want to know when the summer collection drops. When I get an email from that store, I flag the email as coming from a "safe sender." Only I decide who is a safe sender for me. And I can decide, based on the emails coming from that sender, whether they need to be removed from my safe senders list.

I trust you see where I'm going here. You've got lots of people in your life. Likely they should not all be on the safe senders list. You should know, heading into a dinner party, to have your guard up against snarky remarks from that one annoying uncle. He isn't in your safe senders list. You don't volunteer personal information to him. He may have found out your good news through the grapevine, and he may give you some kind of subtle put-down, and you are prepared for it. It's not going to ruin your night. You can ignore him, confront him, or deflect the comment. Your number one concern is to take care of yourself.

I know a lot of people will make you feel guilty if you don't put Uncle Snarky in his place every time he takes a jab. Some people will make you feel that you are weak if you simply deflect the comment or change the subject or ignore the remark altogether. But that's not true. Sometimes, it just isn't worth it. Sometimes, you might not have enough fuel in your tank for the argument that would follow. There is nothing wrong with guarding your peace by avoiding a conversation with a cynical person. The truth is some people will always be cynical. It isn't your job to change them. Keep your distance, as much as possible, and guard your peace by all means. Do not feel obligated to correct every fool you meet. Sometimes the best thing you can do is smile and walk away with your peace intact.

And hey, if you're up for a little confrontation, go for it. Call them out. Maybe flexing that confrontation muscle is exactly what you need. I'm here for all of it!

Susie loves difficult people. I know that seems strange but it's true. My wife's secret to appreciating difficult people is this: she gets curious. She asks herself, "What was this person like as a child?" She says it gives her more empathy for them. She also thinks to herself, "What happened to you? What happened to make you this angry or cynical?"

I asked her why this helps. She said, "I don't take their words personally because I know this has nothing to do with me and everything to do with them." When she looks at a person through the lens of curiosity and compassion, she has way more patience for difficult people. She is also able to not take their hurtful words personally. She says, "Their mean comments have nothing to do with me. That meanness is inside of them. They are being tormented by it. And I feel sorry for them. I may choose to keep my distance, but I do so from a place of empathy and compassion rather than from a place of judgment. It has given me so much peace over the years." There is a lot of wisdom there.

Friendships at Work

Some people believe that the workplace is strictly for business and that socializing with colleagues is unproductive and even a waste of time. But research shows that having friendships at work can actually boost productivity and improve overall job satisfaction.

A study reported on by *Harvard Business Review* found that employees who have close friendships at work are seven times more likely to be engaged in their jobs, leading to higher productivity and better performance. The study also found that people who have close friends at work are more likely to stay with their company long-term, reducing turnover rates and saving the company money on hiring and training costs.

Gallup conducted a survey of fifteen million workers and asked them if they had a close friend at work. They defined "close friend" as someone you can talk to about your personal life. Sadly, only one in three workers had a close friend at work. But those who did were significantly more likely to engage customers and internal partners, get more done in less time, support a safe workplace with fewer accidents and reliability concerns, innovate and share ideas, and have fun while at work.

We have to stop thinking of our social lives as being separate from our work lives. We need to embrace a more holistic approach to work and life. We are in the midst of a loneliness epidemic and it's time to reach out and connect with each other.

GET ALL FIRED UP!

Optimize mental wellness: We all need a support network outside our immediate family. Identify three people to be your safe contacts. If you don't have three people you can ask just yet, start with one and build on that.

Ignite joy: Set a healthy boundary with someone who doesn't make your safe senders list. Although it may sound counterintuitive, you might find taking care of yourself this way is a pleasure.

Fuel peak performance: Friendships at work fuel high performance. Who could you connect with? Invite that person for a coffee or a walk and plan to get to know them better.

10
FACING FAILURE

The only real mistake is the one from which we learn nothing.

HENRY FORD

THE FIRST time I fell in love, I was nine years old. The object of my affection was not a girl. Or a boy. It was music. Rap music. I heard two songs that changed my life: "I Can't Live Without My Radio" by LL Cool J and "Parents Just Don't Understand" by the Fresh Prince. I was smitten. I would play those songs on repeat—and keep in mind, this was 1988. We're talking cassette tapes. Walkmans. To replay a song, you had to press stop, press rewind, try to guess how far back you should go, press stop again, press play, check your progress, and fine-tune your efforts. Listening to a song on repeat took work.

One weekend, I wrote down all the lyrics to "I Can't Live Without My Radio," then I went to school and started rapping the song at recess. Some kids didn't know the song, and I told them I had written it. They were impressed. Was I lying? Yes. But I was also forecasting my future. I was going to be a rapper.

I started writing my own raps at age twelve. I got serious and made my way into a studio at age twenty. I recorded a couple of songs that didn't make it anywhere. Luckily, I was working as an actor at the time—commercials, small roles in TV shows—nothing major, but I was making a living with my acting career and writing raps in my spare time.

I fell in love for a second time at age twenty-three—this time it was a girl. Her name was Susie. We got married at twenty-four, and we're still together now. She's the best thing that ever happened to me. And, unlike rap, she didn't break my heart.

I released a couple of small rap projects in my twenties, but nothing took off. By my late twenties, my acting career had tapered off, and I started working as a motivational speaker in schools. And I would rap in all my presentations. Speaking was so fun—it combined my love of performing on stage with my love of rap music all while spreading a positive message about some of my favorite topics—bullying, mental health, and diversity. I had a new career.

I kept this up throughout my thirties. And every couple of years I would scrape together enough money to rent a studio, hire a producer, and put out a new rap song. I wanted to use my platform as a speaker to build an audience for my rap music. I wrote a song about empathy that got ten thousand views on YouTube. Not bad! I wrote another song about bullying that got forty thousand views on YouTube. Even better! I performed these songs in hundreds of schools, and the feedback was amazing. I was getting closer and closer to my dream of becoming a rapper.

I'll be honest, this dream took way longer than I had hoped it would—I was nearing forty! No rapper that I know of has ever begun their career at age forty. Some would say it's too late. But one thing you need to know about me is that I'm a dreamer. I don't care who says it's too late. I don't care who says it's impossible. If I have a dream, I'm going for it.

When I was forty-two, married with two kids, and living in California, I was finally ready for my big launch as a rap artist. I recorded the best song I've ever written, called "Happy Place." I filmed the best music video I could afford. I had the song professionally mastered by the same team that worked on Pharrell Williams's "Happy." This was going to be my biggest release yet.

I released "Happy Place" in August 2021. And unlike my earlier work, it didn't get forty thousand views. It didn't get ten thousand views. It got... sixty.

Not sixty thousand views. Sixty. A six followed by zero. Less than a hundred. It was a total failure. And it hurt. Badly.

I've heard psychologists talk about the effect of a near miss, when you come so close to a goal that you want to try again. Like those scratcher lottery games that give you a feeling of being very close to winning, even if you lose. They know if you're close to a win, you'll try again.

This song was not a near miss. This song was a complete miss. An utter failure. And I was crushed.

I've had a bunch of failures in my life. But this one was different. This was catastrophic. This was a goal I had pursued for literally *thirty* years! My identity was wrapped in it. It was my childhood dream. And it ended in flames. I was devastated. I went through the worst shame spiral I have ever experienced. I had told everyone I know about the song. And they were all seeing what a failure it was. I realize now that most people are busy worrying about their own life—they aren't thinking about me! But at the time, I felt like crawling into a hole and staying there for weeks.

You might not have dreams of being a rapper. But I bet you've experienced failure. I bet you know what it feels like to hide from people that know about your failure.

Have you ever not answered your phone because of shame?

Have you ever declined an invitation to an event and stayed home because of shame?

Have you ever hidden behind a car in the parking lot of a Mexican restaurant because someone from a team you led drove in and you couldn't face them because of the shame you felt for being the leader on a failed project?

I know I'm not the only one. OK, maybe that last example was just me, but I know you know the sting of shame. It's a sting that delivers a very clear message.

You're not good enough.

Never try that again.
Don't share your art with anyone.
Don't put yourself out there!
Don't share your ideas in a team meeting.
Play small.
Stay safe.
And that's exactly how I felt.

I felt an overwhelming sense of hopelessness. I lost my sense of purpose. Chasing my dream had energized me. Now that my dream had come to an end, I felt like a pilot without a plane. I was lost.

I wish I could tell you I bounced back after a couple of weeks, but this failure sent me spiraling for about a year. I had bouts of anxiety and depression. I had overwhelming feelings of hopelessness. It was awful.

It occurs to me that all of this may sound silly. I mean, I wanted to be a rapper and I failed. Talk about a first-world problem. But keep in mind, this wasn't about the music career that didn't work out. This was about my identity. What I learned most from this failure is the importance of not tying your identity to your success or failure in any given endeavor. Let me unpack some of the other insights I gained from the pain of failure.

Recipe for Disaster

Here's a surefire recipe for shame, depression, and humiliation. This works every time!

1. Convince yourself that your value as a human being is tied to the world's opinion of your work.

2. Release any of that work to the world.

3. Read the comments on social media.

4 Ignore the positive comments.

5 Meditate on the negative ones.

You see, it doesn't matter if it's a music career, or asking someone on a date, or sharing your ideas in a business meeting, or pitching a joke in a writing room. If your self-worth is tied to someone else's opinion, you are entering a world of pain. (Yes, that's a *Big Lebowski* reference. And no, Smokey's toe was not over the line.)

Don't Make Failure Personal

Psychologist Martin Seligman cautions people not to view failure as personal (failure is an event, not a person; do not make the mistake of thinking *you* are a failure); permanent (failure is temporary; do not make the mistake of thinking a failure will last forever); or pervasive (failure is in one area; do not make the mistake of thinking a failure is impacting every area of your life).

If you believe that failure is personal (I'm a failure), permanent (this failure will haunt me for the rest of my life), and pervasive (this failure will destroy my friendships and my career and my love life and my family and my health), you will be overwhelmed with hopelessness. Keep failure in context: You failed at an isolated event. You can move on and still be successful. This reminds me of one of my favorite quotes about failure: "Success is stumbling from failure to failure with no loss of enthusiasm." Thank you, Winston Churchill.

Don't "Doom-Scroll" on Social Media

Here's a bad idea: scroll through social media and compare your recent loss with everyone else's victories. I had to take a huge step back from social media to recover from my failure. Every time I scrolled through my feed, I would feel like such a loser. Pay attention to how you feel about yourself after you've spent time online. Is it helping, or hurting? If it's getting in the way of you recovering from your setback, consider deleting the app from your phone for a month or two.

Learning in the School of Hard Knocks

Stanford psychologist Carol Dweck teaches the difference between a growth mindset and a fixed mindset. Let's say you're a student and you failed a math test. A fixed mindset says, "I am bad at math," and looks at that test as evidence. A growth mindset says, "If I study the questions I got wrong, I can get better at math!" and uses that test as an opportunity for growth and improvement. Every failure, whether it be a relationship, a business, or a creative venture, has something to teach us. Be open to the lessons to be learned after failure! The tuition is high, but failure can be a great teacher!

Even Small Wins Are a Big Deal

We are in the midst of a burnout epidemic. People are leaving their jobs or "quiet quitting" at never-before-seen rates. There are many reasons for this, but I'm only going to mention one...

Employees are not being celebrated for their efforts.

Sure, if you're the employee of the month, you'll get your picture on the wall. But celebrating small wins, and acknowledging effort, goes a long way in giving people a sense of joy and accomplishment at work. One of the antidotes to burnout is employee recognition.

What if you work for yourself? Even if you're a solopreneur, celebrating your small wins is crucial. Burnout and frustration can result from waiting to see how your work is received by clients or the marketplace. Much more regenerative and life-giving is to set a goal within your control and celebrate the fact that you reached that goal.

For example, let's say your goal is to write a *New York Times* bestseller. You can't control whether your book lands on that coveted list. But you can control whether you write five hundred words a day, three times a week. I think it's a much better idea to set a word count goal and then focus on hitting that goal as your measure of success. Forget how the book is received. Celebrate the victory of writing five hundred words a day!

This is why I love the book *Atomic Habits* by James Clear. His big idea is to focus on your system rather than your goal. If you go out for a run today, celebrate that small win! Every time I do a workout, whether it's a short run or some serious weightlifting, at the end of my workout I say, "This is the promise I keep to myself." I did it. I did it. Yes! That is the win! It's not stepping on the scale to see if you lost weight. Don't look in the mirror. Just celebrate the fact that you did what you said you were going to do.

Focus on what you can control. You can't control whether your book is a bestseller. But you can control whether you finish the manuscript. So, reframe success!

Success is publishing your blog post, not seeing how many times your blog post was shared on social media.

Success is making one hundred cold calls, not booking three sales meetings.

Success is releasing your music video, not getting a million views.

Success is asking your crush on a date, regardless of their response.

Keep failure in context: you failed at an isolated event. **You can move on and still be successful.**

Success is asking for a promotion, no matter the outcome.

Focus on what you can control. And be consistent. Get feedback from failures. Get feedback from successes. Adjust your strategy and keep playing the game.

Celebrate the small wins! Buy a bottle of champagne and keep it in the fridge. That's the bottle that gets opened when you finish the manuscript.

Maybe you buy a gift card to a spa. And you only get to go to the spa when you finish those cold calls.

Maybe it's a fancy ice cream.

But you've got to celebrate. Make it a big deal.

What can managers do with their department? A party? Fancy donuts? In the TV show *Severance*, all they get when they hit their quota is a lousy melon party. Melons? I think you can do better!

If you're in charge of a department and you're working on a project, celebrate the achievement of getting the work done. Make it a big deal. Don't wait to see how anyone else receives it.

So now I know where I went wrong. I released my song into the world and then held my breath to see what everyone would think. I should have had a party! I should have released the song and then jumped into a hot tub with a glass of champagne! I should have had a small party with friends and just celebrated the fact that I had the courage to share my work with the world.

From now on, in any creative endeavor I work on, I will build in small wins and big parties as I progress on the goals I can control! Pop that champagne!

Burnout

You don't see it coming. That's the sneaky thing with burnout. When my kids were three and four years old, I was burning the candle at both ends. Working nights and weekends, long days, long nights, it was endless. And I didn't hit my breaking point. But shortly after the Covid lockdowns ended, I found myself jumpy and irritable, and exhausted with a tiredness that coffee couldn't touch. I found everyone and everything unbearable. I hit burnout.

The weird part was that my workdays were actually shorter. I wasn't working nights or weekends. And my kids, now teens, were less demanding. So why did I hit burnout then? If you consider all the stressors I had ten years before, I should have burnt out then. Not now. The math didn't add up. And that's what I kept telling myself.

This doesn't make sense.

I should be able to power through this.

Why can't I keep going?

What's wrong with me?

If you are looking for ways to recover from burnout, do not add guilt and shame to your plate. What you need now is self-compassion. And then to recognize the steps in recovering from burnout.

Three Steps for Recovery from Burnout

Step one: Accept that you are, in fact, experiencing burnout.

When I finally realized what I had been feeling for weeks, I was relieved. The truth is the only way out of burnout is to go all the way through it. And the first step is to acknowledge that you are burnt out. Own it. Admit it. To borrow from the addiction and recovery community, step one in the journey is acceptance.

Step two: Tell someone.

For me, this meant I had to tell Susie. I told her how I was feeling. I told her I felt like a failure for feeling this way. I told her I felt weak. She had been asking me what was wrong, and I kept avoiding it, but now it all came out. And I will be honest, I cried a lot. A good cry is great for your mental health.

A quick word for my fellow brothers who may have a tough time crying. Did you know that when you cry, your body releases stress hormones through your tears? It's true. When you slice onions, your eyes produce tears that have no stress hormones in them. But when you cry from heartache, your body physically processes those emotions by releasing stress hormones through your tears. It's amazing. Scientifically speaking, crying makes perfect logical sense. Holding back tears, on the other hand, is completely illogical. When you refuse to cry, you are working against the chemistry of your own body. I had a good cry with Susie that day. And I felt much better afterward.

Step three: Strategize for recovery.

Burnout should be a wake-up call: something must change. The current system isn't working, and you need an overhaul. As the old saying goes, "If you keep doing what you're doing, you'll keep getting what you're getting." You've got to take your recovery seriously. Reduce all but the most necessary activities. Think of yourself as on triage. Only the most essential tasks will be done. Everything else must be eliminated. You need three things: rest, rest, and more rest.

I had to place self-care at the top of my priority list. For me, the number one focus of my self-care strategy was sleep. I prioritized getting eight hours of sleep a night, every night. Even if that meant that we needed to cancel plans, nothing was going to be a higher priority than sleep. We had a family meeting, and I told my kids that I was overtired, and I needed to get more sleep, and starting that day, I would be unavailable after 9:45 pm. That one decision was a game-changer for me. We talked about sleep in chapter 7, but it is worth repeating. Nothing has a more profound impact on your mood, energy levels, and overall wellness than sleep.

Rehab for Burnout

Recovering from burnout is a lot like recovering from an injury. If you try to rush your healing, you'll end up aggravating your injury and prolonging the recovery period. It seems counterintuitive but it's true: the slower you go, the faster you progress. You want to slow your life all the way down. You might have a day, or a few hours in a day, when you feel like yourself. You'll be tempted to take on some huge project. But a word to the wise: slow down. Think of yourself like an injured athlete who is in rehab. Even if they feel better, they won't get back to full speed right away.

An excellent question to keep asking yourself is "What do I need now?" Care for yourself as you would a child for whom you are responsible. If that child had, for whatever reason, reached exhaustion, what would you say? Would you shame the child? Would you make the child feel guilty for trying too hard at school or playing too hard in a sport? Or would you shower the child with unconditional love and support? Take care of yourself the same way, especially when you're burnt out.

Now, before we end this chapter, I have one important question I'd like to ask you…

What Does the Voice in Your Head Say?

When you make a mistake, what does your inner voice sound like? Some of us have an inner critic that is far too harsh. And when you're dealing with failure and burnout, self-compassion is critical. You've got to treat yourself with care. Talk to yourself like you'd talk to a friend.

Imagine this: Your friend calls you. They had a horrible day at work because they forgot some important material for a big presentation. They tell you that they feel like an idiot. What would you say to your friend?

Would you agree with them and call them an idiot?
Would you ask them why they are so irresponsible?
Would you berate them for being so forgetful?

I hope the answer is no! I hope you would comfort them and offer them support and encouragement. I hope you would say something along the lines of...

You're not an idiot—I've done the same thing!
Don't be so hard on yourself—you're human!
But now let's reverse the roles...

If you forget some important material for a big presentation, how do you speak to yourself? Do you call yourself an idiot? Pay attention to your inner voice. Ask yourself: If I spoke to my friends the way I speak to myself, would I still have any friends? As high performers, we have high expectations of ourselves. And that's good. Yes, we should learn from our mistakes. Yes, we should do better next time. But when it comes to recovering from failure, self-compassion is far more effective than self-flagellation.

GET ALL FIRED UP!

Optimize mental wellness: A failure does not mean you're finished. Bookmark this chapter and the next time you experience a failure, reread it to remind yourself your best days are still in front of you.

Ignite joy: Practice celebrating small wins. It doesn't matter how small. Here's an idea: Buy yourself a bath bomb. Choose one item on your to-do list that requires some extra effort, and know that when you tick it off, you're going to celebrate with a soothing, fragrant soak.

Fuel peak performance: The next time you make a mistake, treat yourself with the compassion you would offer a friend.

11

EXCUSE-LESS

Success is the sum of small efforts, repeated day in and day out.

ROBERT COLLIER

YOU'VE REACHED the last chapter. This one is all about motivation and productivity. First off, let me start by saying that being productive is not about being busy all the time. It's about making the most of your time and energy to achieve your goals and fulfill your purpose. And I get really excited about being productive.

My happiest days are my most productive days. Every evening, I find myself looking back over the day to see how well I managed my time. I get a little boost if I did any of the following:

- Spent time with my loved ones
- Had a good day at work
- Made progress on a creative project
- Exercised/moved my body
- Connected with my faith in a meaningful way
- Helped another person or served my community
- Cooked, cleaned, or shopped for groceries
- Practiced breathing exercises and/or meditation

If I get a handful of those things done in a day, I feel on top of the world! I can spend the evening totally relaxed because I feel a sense of accomplishment. I absolutely love the feeling of knowing I had a balanced, productive day. I feel connected to my purpose. I feel a sense of momentum, I'm moving in the right direction with my life. I love that feeling! Don't you?

On the flip side, if I don't get anything on the above list done in a day, I feel miserable. I feel lost. I feel disconnected from purpose. The simple truth is, I am at my best when I am intentional about how I spend my time. I think the same is true for all of us.

A Working Definition of Success

Earl Nightingale defined success as "the progressive realization of a worthy goal." We can adapt that to say that success is gradual progress toward a worthwhile goal. I love those two words: gradual progress. Success is taking small steps in the direction of your dream. You want to learn a new language? You might not be able to read a novel in Spanish this evening, but you can take one Spanish class online today. If you do that, you are moving in the direction of your goals. And that is a big deal. A lot of people have dreams, but very few people take small, purposeful steps toward those dreams. That leads us to some critical questions.

1 What are your goals?
2 What can you do today to get where you want to be in the future?

Do you want to write a screenplay? Do you want a great marriage? Do you want to save enough money for a down payment on a house? Do you want to hit a certain sales target? You can't hit a goal if you haven't defined it. The little steps today will take you to your destiny. There is no sense in dreaming big if you aren't willing to start small. But if you commit to daily, incremental progress, there is no limit to what you can achieve.

Little by Little

You can't determine whether you've had a productive, successful day if you don't have any goals. And to be honest, setting goals and chasing after them is fun. You feel the thrill of the chase. You feel a rush of accomplishment when you hit your goal. And the more days you hit that goal, the more fuel in your tank for the next day. You end up building this incredible momentum in your life. That's what I want for you. But it all starts with setting a goal, breaking that goal down into manageable chunks, and measuring your progress. Small, incremental gains lead to massive change.

I am always blown away by how much you can get done little by little. The book you are holding is an example of that. When I first set out to write it, I stopped myself several times because "I don't have the time."

I pictured a solitary writer holed up in a cabin in the woods for a couple of months and emerging with a manuscript. I didn't have a couple of months to dedicate to writing a book... and I didn't have a cabin in the woods! But I did have a few hours in my week that I could set aside for writing. And that's what I did. It took me about eight months—and of course, it would take me a bit longer to rewrite, edit, publish, and get it out into the world. That first week, all I had to show for my efforts was about a page and a half of ideas. But that's how every book is written, one sentence at a time.

As the creativity expert Julia Cameron has observed, "The 'if I had time' lie is a convenient way to ignore the fact that novels require being written and that writing happens a sentence at a time. Sentences can happen in a moment. Enough stolen moments, enough stolen sentences, and a novel is born—without the luxury of time."

To borrow another quote from the inspirational Earl Nightingale, "Don't let the fear of the time it will take to accomplish something stand in the way of your doing it. The time will pass anyway; we might just as well put that passing time to the best possible use."

So, here's how I tackled the project you are holding in your hand. I set my goal—"I want to write a book." Then I put together a plan to reach that goal and a way to measure my progress.

How to tackle a project in three simple steps:
1. Set a goal.
2. Make a plan.
3. Measure your progress.

I researched online and learned that a short nonfiction book could be about thirty thousand words. Now I needed to break down how much I could do in a single day. Here's something I learned from James Clear, author of the fantastic book *Atomic Habits*: "Motivation comes and goes. If you want to do something consistently, then don't pick a level of difficulty that requires great motivation. Make it easy enough and simple enough that you'll do it even when you don't feel very motivated."

Don't make a commitment based on what you can get done on a good day, make a commitment based on what you can get done on a bad day. On a good day, I can write one thousand words. That's about two typed pages, single-spaced, at twelve-point font. On a bad day, I can write about half that, five hundred words. If I'm in a groove and I write more than five hundred words—that's fantastic! But I'd much rather set the bar low and hit it every time, rather than set the bar too high and wear myself out. There will be days when you get a flat tire and your favorite team loses and your kid throws up on your shoes on the way to work. What can you commit to even on a day like that? For me, it's writing five hundred words. That became my commitment for writing days.

You feel a rush of accomplishment when you hit your goal. **And the more days you hit that goal, the more fuel in your tank for the next day.**

I did the math: Thirty thousand words divided by five hundred words per day equals sixty days. I need sixty writing days to finish a manuscript. It's amazing how breaking a big challenge down into manageable chunks can get you fired up!

Now sixty writing days do not equal two months. No, no, no. I want balance in my life. I don't want to work on weekends. I also knew I didn't want to be forced to write five days a week. I needed some research days and some days off. So I decided to commit to writing three days a week, five hundred words per day.

I did more math: Five hundred words a day times three days a week equals 1,500 words per week. Thirty thousand words divided by 1,500 words equals twenty weeks. Life happens, so I added four weeks on top of that. I gave myself twenty-four weeks to write the book. That's a plan. That's something I can measure. That's something I can check in to see if I'm progressing on or not.

Looking at my calendar and counting those weeks put a fire under my seat. But that fire wasn't enough. Once I had a realistic deadline, I needed to be accountable to others!

Social Pressure

It's one thing to have a deadline that no one else knows about. But as soon as you tell people about your deadline, the pressure is real! So I told my closest friends that I was writing a book. I told them about the timeline. And I asked them to follow up with me to see how it was going. Now I had a deadline and some accountability for that deadline. For me, knowing my friends were going to ask me about my progress was enough stress to get me going on days I didn't feel like writing.

How about you? Are projects sitting dormant in your mind? Could you use accountability to your advantage by giving yourself a deadline and some social pressure? It sure works for me! The book you are holding is proof!

Temptation Bundling

In her book *How to Change,* Katy Milkman introduces a concept called "temptation bundling." It's a clever technique where you couple a task you aren't particularly fond of with something you genuinely enjoy. For instance, you could listen to your favorite podcast only while tidying up your home, treat yourself to a sauna session only post-workout, or blast your favorite playlist only during exercise. The goal is to inject a little fun into otherwise mundane activities. Go ahead, give it a try!

Lagging Indicators

A lagging indicator is a measurement that reflects past behavior. Your current credit score is a lagging indicator of your past credit behavior. If you shift your credit behavior this afternoon, you won't see a change in your credit score tomorrow. But if you are consistent with better borrowing habits, a few months down the road your credit score will reflect your good behavior. Your good or bad choices take time to show up in your life. That's what makes it a *lagging* indicator.

Why are lagging indicators such a big deal? Sometimes, we get so discouraged by looking at where we are now that we lose all motivation to make any meaningful change. We look at the extra weight, the thousands of dollars of debt, or the hurt we've caused a loved one and we think our situation is hopeless. But it's not hopeless, it's just a lagging indicator of decisions made in the past. The good news is you can change it! You can commit to small steps today and you will see a brand-new set of lagging indicators down the road. What small steps do you need to take today?

Maybe it's spending a little more quality time with a loved one each day.

Maybe it's packing a lunch instead of buying takeout.

Maybe it's saving 10 percent of your income.

Maybe it's having dessert on weekends only.

Maybe it's exercising three days a week.

These little choices won't make a difference today. But if you stick with them, they make a tremendous difference in your life. Incremental improvements add up to gigantic gains. As the famous Chinese proverb says, "The journey of a thousand miles begins with a single step." Have the courage to take that single step!

Success on Your Own Terms

We defined success as gradual progress toward a worthwhile goal. That word "worthwhile" is key. Because only you can decide what is worthwhile. I can't tell you how you should be spending your time. That's got to come from you and you alone. You are the only person on earth who decides what success looks like for you. But whatever it is, I want you to be successful! And I hope this book is a little extra fuel for your journey.

GET ALL FIRED UP!

Optimize mental wellness: What does a successful day look like for you? Make a list of the top five to seven things you need to do in a day to feel successful. Get into the habit of reviewing the list at the end of the day.

Ignite joy: Identify a current big dream or goal. Be *ambitious* with your goal. Feel the thrill of imagining yourself accomplishing it. That should put fuel in your tank for the journey ahead!

Fuel peak performance: Write out a plan that breaks down the goal into small steps. Be *realistic* with your time and capacity.

Find out who you are
and do it on purpose.

DOLLY PARTON

CONCLUSION

THIS BOOK is your reminder that if you want to be your best at work and at home, you've got to prioritize your mental wellness. What does that look like?

Maybe it means you practice box breathing before you transition from work life to home life.

Maybe it means you take a long hot bath before bed.

Maybe it means you book a massage once a month.

Maybe it means you hire a babysitter (or do a babysitting swap with another family) once every two weeks so you can go on a date with your partner.

Maybe it means you go on a long walk every day during your lunch break. (As a reminder, a lunch break is a break from work to enjoy food and recreation. If you want to get serious about your mental wellness, lunch breaks are a great place to start!)

Life is hard. You need to recharge. And that, in and of itself, is reason enough for you to prioritize your own wellness. But there are side effects.

When you sleep more, you perform better at work.

When you practice self-care, you have more patience with your family.

When you indulge in laughter and joy, you become more creative in problem-solving.

When you practice meditation, prayer, mindfulness, and breathwork, you build an internal reservoir that you can draw from during times of adversity.

The benefits of prioritizing your mental wellness are incredible. Your family will thank you for it. Your team at work will thank you for it. Your partner will thank you for it. But you aren't doing it for them. You are doing it for yourself. And that, in and of itself, is enough.

ACKNOWLEDGMENTS

NEVER COULD have written this book without the support of some truly incredible people in my life. First, as always, is my life partner, my soulmate, my beautiful wife, Susie McLean. When we took our vows, we promised to support each other in our dreams. That's what we've been doing all these years and I think it's the most beautiful thing in the world. You've seen me at my best, and you've seen me at my worst, and your love has never changed. You are the greatest blessing in my life and I thank God for you! Now put down this book and let's go for a walk in Toluca Lake and dream about our future.

To our amazing kids—sorry, teens—Josh and Ariella, I am so proud of who you are and the way you navigate through life. I am always honored to introduce you to anyone—these are my kids, look how incredible they are! Keep shining you two!

Huge thanks to my all-star booking team at Speakers' Spotlight. Martin and Farah Perelmuter, you gave me a platform and opened doors for me to speak to audiences around the world. And we're just getting started! Huge shoutout to the entire team that screens emails, books flights, coordinates logistics, preps sound, troubleshoots everything, and allows me to show up on stage and focus on one thing: speaking. Truly, I am grateful to all of you: Ream Badawi, Marnie Ballane, Elise Bercovici-Diker, Michelle Bertol-Bone, Alexa Breininger, Jemimah Cataga, Erica Conrad, Courtney Cooper, Alannah Ford, Kristen Gentleman, Kelly Hutton, Dwight Ireland, Kelly MacDonald, Catherine McCabe, Marta Moher, Bryce Moloney, Jane Panasiuk, Amy Panchyshyn, Cindy Paredes, Mélanie Roy, Paula Sage, Holly Santandrea, Cindy Sheridan, Zoila Solomon, Paul Terefenko, Kelli Thompson, Emily Wannamaker, Aya Xamin, and Michelle Xu.

And huge thanks to Marianne Woods at Talk About Speakers! You believed in me before I ever spoke for a corporate audience. You took a chance on me and gave me life-changing opportunities. I'll never forget that. Thanks, Marianne!

To my mom! You believed in this project from the moment I told you about it. I never could have done this without your support. Thanks for cheering me on from page one all the way through to the last chapter. Love you now and always!

To my family—McLeans, Smalleys, Vandenbrinks, Bankses, Cotterells, Browns, Faceys—you are the invisible support system behind me every time I stand up to speak. I'm so thankful for the bond we share! Love you all!

To my sister, Kate Smalley—conversations with you have bloomed into lifestyle changes and new habits and material in this book. I love you. I admire you. You radiate warmth, wisdom, and joy. Seriously, you are amazing.

To my brother, Andrew McLean—you've been a rock in my life through the toughest times I've ever been through. Thanks for being a lighthouse when I felt lost at sea. Love you now. Love you forever.

To my stepmother, Blossom McLean—so thankful for your optimism, your positivity, your hope for the future through everything life throws at you. You are the face of perseverance and I love you so much!

To my sister-in-law Lucy Vandenbrink—I'm so thankful for the wisdom you lent to this book! Your insight into anxiety and somatics have been invaluable! You have inspired me to be a lifelong learner in the wellness space.

To my dear friend, Meghan Warby—you are one of the most generous human beings I have ever met. Thank you for taking the time to work through sections of this book line by line with me. And I love the community of screenwriters we are building between LA and Toronto!

To my friends in LA and my friends in Toronto! Thanks for all the deep conversations, the belly laughs, the embarrassing memories, and the fun that is to come. For insight into this book, special thanks to Sherien Barsoum, Dave and Morgan Hansow, Andrew and Emily Sorlie, Curtis Carmichael, Chris Cummins, Viktor and Diana Atkins, Sue and Christian Martinsen, Emily Hazel, Jonathan Puddle, Max Spransy, Tierney Michon, Tara Stephenson, Kendall Myers, Belinda Huang, Stan and Amy Min, Josh and Sarah McCarron, Sandra and Miguel Khan, Mike and Sara Reventar, Duane Forrest, Germaine Ransome, Joel Witton, Shonna Foster, Savio Joseph, Caleb and Chloe MacDonald, Alicia Richardson, Emily and Blake Fleischacker, Jason and Gillian Schuler, Jordan Bigler, Tinasha LaRayé, Kev and Gill Lea, Timothy Miller, Donna Hynes, Susan Driediger, Robyn Foyle, Trent Monroe, Kate and Isaac Rentz, Seth and Heidi Richardson, Auston Copeland, Ed and Hannah Flint, and the whole community at Bread Church in LA. Love y'all!

Finally, a huge thanks to the team at Page Two for walking me through the journey of how to write, edit, market, and distribute this book. I was so overwhelmed and intimidated when this project began, but from my first conversation with Jesse Finkelstein (you rock!) I knew I was in good hands with

Page Two! My journey started with an ongoing collaboration with fellow author Emily Schultz, who gave me the confidence to find my voice on the page. Thank you to Louise Hill for her gentle yet persistent nudges in getting me to my deadlines! My design meeting with Jennifer Lum got me fired up to rethink elements of the manuscript and I learned a tremendous amount about marketing from Ariell Hudnall. My copy editor, Rachel Taylor, was thoughtful and thorough and I owe her a debt of gratitude! A very special thanks to my editor Kendra Ward. You saw the diamonds in the rough manuscript I gave you, and you helped me to bring this book to life. Thank you for your care and attention to every page in this book. I couldn't have done it without you!

And to you, dear reader! Thank you for buying this book. I hope it gives you fuel to live your best life!

NOTES

xv *In 2021, an estimated one in five adults* "Mental Illness," National Institute of Mental Health, www.nimh.nih.gov/health/statistics/mental-illness. This page provides comprehensive information about the prevalence of mental illnesses among adults in the US.

10 *The group that practiced meditation* Julia C. Basso et al., "Brief, Daily Meditation Enhances Attention, Memory, Mood, and Emotional Regulation in Non-experienced Meditators," *Behavioural Brain Research* 356, no. 1 (January 2019): 208–20, doi.org/10.1016/j.bbr.2018.08.023.

13 *Numerous studies have proven* Kirsten Weir, "Nurtured by Nature," *Monitor on Psychology* 51, no. 3 (April/May 2020): n.p. [print version: p. 50], American Psychological Association, www.apa.org/monitor/2020/04/nurtured-nature.

13 *And medical researchers have proven* Holger C. Bringmann et al., "Mantra Meditation as Adjunctive Therapy in Major Depression: A Randomized Controlled Trial," *Journal of Affective Disorders Reports* 6 (December 2021): n.p., doi.org/10.1016/j.jadr.2021.100232.

22 *The group that took breaks* Atsunori Ariga and Alejandro Lleras, "Brief and Rare Mental 'Breaks' Keep You Focused: Deactivation and Reactivation of Task Goals Preempt Vigilance Decrements," *Developmental Cell* 18, no. 3 (March 2010): 439–43, doi.org/10.1016/j.cognition.2010.12.007.

24 *Since Covid began* "Remote Work Since COVID-19 Is Exacerbating Harm," Project Include, March 2021, projectinclude.org/assets/pdf/Project-Include-Harassment-Report-0321-F3.pdf.

25 *She teaches that there are different types of rest* Dr. Saundra Dalton-Smith, *Sacred Rest: Recover Your Life, Renew Your Energy, Restore Your Sanity* (FaithWords, December 2017).

29 *One survey found that 60 percent* Paychex, *2021 State of Mental Health in the Workplace Report* (Paychex, 2021), https://www.paychex.com/sites/default/files/2021-04/mental_health_report_0.pdf.

36 *In fact, according to a study by the Mayo Clinic* "Stress Relief From Laughter? It's No Joke," In-Depth, Mayo Clinic, July 29, 2021, www.mayoclinic.org/healthy-lifestyle/stress-management/in-depth/stress-relief/art-20044456.

37 *The patients who were watching comedies* Edinara Moraes Morais, Paulo Ricardo Moreira, and Eliane Roseli Winkelmann, "Movie Watching During Dialysis Sessions Reduces Depression and Anxiety and Improves Quality of Life: A Randomized Clinical Trial," *Complementary Therapies in Medicine* 52 (August 2020), doi.org/10.1016/j.ctim.2020.102488.

37 *Another study proved* American Physiological Society, "Anticipating a Laugh Reduces Our Stress Hormones, Study Shows," Science News, ScienceDaily, April 10, 2008, www.sciencedaily.com/releases/2008/04/080407114617.htm.

43 *But author Joline Godfrey* Joline Godfrey quoted in Apata Oyeniran, "Chrisland Schools: Aiding Students' Devt through Extra-Curricular Activities," Independent.ng, July 6, 2022, independent.ng/chrisland-schools-aiding-students-devt-through-extra-curricular-activities/.

43 *Some studies suggest* Lawrence Robinson et al., "The Benefits of Play for Adults," Well-Being & Happiness, HelpGuide, www.helpguide.org/articles/mental-health/benefits-of-play-for-adults.htm.

55 *It's one of the best ways* Ashish Sharma, Vishal Madaan, and Frederick D. Petty, "Exercise for Mental Health," *Primary Care Companion to the Journal of Clinical Psychiatry* 8, no. 2 (2006): 106, doi.org/10.4088/pcc.v08n0208a.

55 *Moving your body* Daniel Preiato and Ryan Collins, "Exercise and the Brain: The Mental Health Benefits of Exercise," Healthline, last updated May 10, 2023, www.healthline.com/health/depression/exercise.

55 *One study showed that intense exercise* University of California–Davis Health System, "This Is Your Brain on Exercise: Vigorous Exercise Boosts Critical Neurotransmitters, May Help Restore Mental Health," Science News, ScienceDaily, February 25, 2016, www.sciencedaily.com/releases/2016/02/160225101241.htm.

56 *Low levels of BDNF* Jungyun Hwang et al., "Acute High-Intensity Exercise-Induced Cognitive Enhancement and Brain-Derived Neurotrophic Factor in Young, Healthy Adults," *Neuroscience Letters* 630 (September 6, 2016): 247–53, doi.org/10.1016/j.neulet.2016.07.033.

57 *Cold showers stimulate* Nikolai A. Shevchuk, "Adapted Cold Shower as a Potential Treatment for Depression," *Medical Hypotheses* 70, no. 5 (2008): 995–1001, doi.org/10.1016/j.mehy.2007.04.052.

57 *The Stanford University School of Medicine* Gül Dölen et al., "Social Reward Requires Coordinated Activity of Nucleus Accumbens Oxytocin and Serotonin," *Nature* 501, no. 7466 (September 2013): 179–84, doi.org/10.1038/nature12518.

58 *It is incredibly effective* Christophe André, "Proper Breathing Brings Better Health," Fitness, *Scientific American*, January 15, 2019, www.scientificamerican.com/article/proper-breathing-brings-better-health/.

58 *So, when you follow breathing patterns* Emma Seppälä, Christina Bradley, and Michael R. Goldstein, "Research: Why Breathing Is So Effective at Reducing Stress," *Harvard Business Review*, September 29, 2020, hbr.org/2020/09/research-why-breathing-is-so-effective-at-reducing-stress.

65 *They found that self-awareness* Ginka Toegel and Jean-Louis Barsoux, "How To Become a Better Leader," *MIT Sloan Management Review*, March 20, 2012, sloanreview.mit.edu/article/how-to-become-a-better-leader/.

65 *Another study, this one of 486 publicly traded companies* David Zes and Dana Landis, "A Better Return on Self-Awareness," *Briefings Magazine* 5, no. 17 (2013/14): 10–12, Korn Ferry, https://www.kornferry.com/content/dam/kornferry/docs/pdfs/Briefings_Issue17.pdf.

84 *One study found that breathing exercises* Bob Yirka, "Study Shows Cyclic Breathing Technique More Effective in Reducing Stress than Mindfulness Meditation," MedicalXpress, January 16, 2023,

medicalxpress.com/news/2023-01-cyclic-technique-effective-stress-mindfulness.html.

94 *Improved mood: Studies have shown* Chiara Baglioni et al., "Insomnia as a Predictor of Depression and Anxiety: A Meta-Analytic Review of Longitudinal Epidemiological Studies," *Journal of Affective Disorders* 135(1–3): 10–19, doi.org/10.1016/j.jad.2011.01.011. In this meta-analytic review, the authors gathered data from twenty-one longitudinal studies and found a strong correlation between insomnia and the development of depression and anxiety. Insomnia was considered a strong predictor of future mental health disorders, underscoring the importance of good sleep for mental health.

96 *Studies have shown that sleep deprivation* "Stress and Sleep," American Psychological Association, 2013, www.apa.org/news/press/releases/stress/2013/sleep.

96 *One study found that people who slept* Amanda Blackwelder, Mikhail Hoskins, and Larissa Huber, "Effect of Inadequate Sleep on Frequent Mental Distress," *Preventing Chronic Disease* 18 (June 17, 2021), doi.org/10.5888/pcd18.200573.

99 *Studies have suggested that adequate* Priscilla Koduah, Friedemann Paul, and Jan-Markus Dörr, "Vitamin D in the Prevention, Prediction and Treatment of Neurodegenerative and Neuroinflammatory Diseases," *EPMA Journal* 8 (2017): 313–25, doi.org/10.1007/s13167-017-0120-8.

117 *When you hug someone* Susanna Newsonen, "The Shocking Truth About Hugs," Stress, *Psychology Today*, March 3, 2022, www.psychologytoday.com/us/blog/the-path-passionate-happiness/202203/the-shocking-truth-about-hugs.

118 *A study at Purdue University* Megan Huckaby, "Study Shows Service Dogs Are Associated with Lower PTSD Symptoms Among War Veterans," News, Purdue University, February 8, 2018, www.purdue.edu/newsroom/releases/2018/Q1/study-shows-service-dogs-are-associated-with-lower-ptsd-symptoms-among-war-veterans-.html.

118 *In 2019, a study of over ten thousand adults* "Loneliness and the Work-place: 2020 US Report," Cigna, January 2020, www.cigna.com/static/www-cigna-com/docs/about-us/newsroom/studies-and-reports/combatting-loneliness/cigna-2020-loneliness-report.pdf.

129 *A study reported on by Harvard Business Review* Jon Clifton, "The Power of Work Friends," *Harvard Business Review*, October 7, 2022, hbr.org/2022/10/the-power-of-work-friends.

129 *Gallup conducted a survey* Alok Patel and Stephanie Plowman, "The Increasing Importance of a Best Friend at Work," Workplace, Gallup, August 17, 2022, www.gallup.com/workplace/397058/increasing-importance-best-friend-work.aspx.

151 *As the creativity expert* Julia Cameron, *The Right to Write: An Invitation and Initiation into the Writing Life* (New York: Jeremy P. Tarcher/Putnam, 1998).

152 *Here's something I learned from James Clear* James Clear, "Motivation, Criticism, and the Goal of Adulthood," 3-2-1 Newsletter, March 24, 2022, jamesclear.com/3-2-1/march-24-2022.

ABOUT THE AUTHOR

JACKSON DAVIS

Called a "master storyteller," Anthony McLean delivers lively, actionable presentations on mental wellness, diversity and inclusion, and the intersection between them. He's worked with such leading organizations as PepsiCo, AT&T, Intel, Danone, Coca-Cola, and more. McLean shows audiences how to foster an environment of empathy, acceptance, and mental well-being to enhance DEI work and optimize individual and team performance.

A respected voice in his field, McLean has delivered hundreds of inspiring talks across the world, rocking the stage at conferences, colleges, and corporate events. His clients have ranged from charities and nonprofits to Fortune 500s. McLean is passionate about education and credits teachers for making the biggest difference in his life. Delivering research-backed tools and actionable strategies, he leaves audiences inspired to bring their best every day.

McLean has a background in theatre and works actively in the film and television industry. As a screenwriter, he's currently in development on two feature films. He lives in Los Angeles, California, with his wife and their two kids.

IGNITE YOUR TEAM'S POTENTIAL!

Looking to steer your team toward peak performance by prioritizing mental wellness? Here's how we can spark that journey!

Invest in Your Team
Purchase copies of *All Fired Up* for your team, and I'll send you a free PDF handout. Use it to guide a meaningful conversation about mental wellness with your team.

Invest in Your Organization
Planning to get copies for your whole organization? Contact me about bulk discounts and special offers, or about developing a custom edition for your organization.

Amplify Your Event
I'm ready to rock the stage at your next event! Let's ignite a passion for mental wellness and peak performance among your attendees. *Let's gooooo!*

Start the Conversation
Visit us online! anthonymclean.org/book
Hit me up on social: @anthonymclean

If you've made it this far into
the book, I'm hoping that means
you've enjoyed what you've read!

In today's world, books like ours have a funny little ritual—the online review. Think of it as a modern version of a round of applause. So, if you could spare a moment to pen a few lines for a review on your favorite online retailer, it would mean the world to me. I appreciate you!

www.ingramcontent.com/pod-product-compliance
Lightning Source LLC
Chambersburg PA
CBHW031110080526
44587CB00011B/913